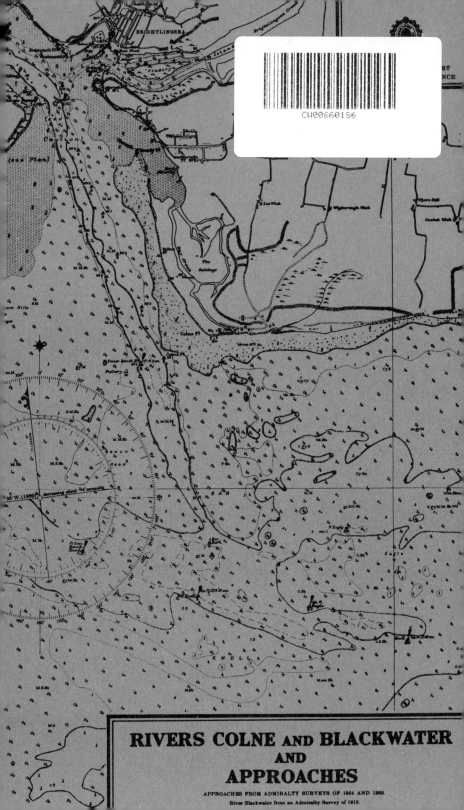

RIVERS COLNE AND BLACKWATER
AND
APPROACHES

APPROACHES FROM ADMIRALTY SURVEYS OF 1954 AND 1965.

River Blackwater from an Admiralty Survey of 1918.

BOADICEA
CK 213

BOADICEA
CK 213

The Story of an
East Coast Fishing Smack

MICHAEL FROST

Illustrated by the author

ANGUS & ROBERTSON

Angus & Robertson
London
Sydney · Singapore · Manila

Endpaper map reproduced from BA chart
no. 3741 with the sanction of the Control-
ler, HM Stationery Office and of the
Hydrographer of the Navy.

First published by
Angus and Robertson (U.K.) Ltd. in 1974
Copyright © Michael Frost 1974
ISBN 0 207 95532 8
Printed in Great Britain by
Northumberland Press Ltd.
Gateshead.

Acknowledgments

During the preparation of this book I have received much help and encouragement and I would like to thank Mr John Lewis, who has described the rebuilding of the smack in his own books. Had it not been for his sustained belief that my log books could be reduced to readable form it is probable that the book would never have been begun, let alone finished, and I am most grateful to him.

I am also very grateful to Mr Christopher Hughes, who read an earlier draft of the book and made many helpful criticisms which helped me in my descriptions and improved the balance of the subject matter.

The pictures for Chapters One and Five were drawn for me by Mr F. B. Harnack from two of his water colours of the period and I am very grateful to him, for his help and for allowing me to use them.

The picture of the Dutch fishing boats in Chapter Seventeen was drawn from a postcard of the period and I am very grateful to de Heer J. C. Dert of Flushing, for allowing me to use it.

Finally, I wish to thank my publishers and, in particular, I am most grateful to Mr Ian Dear, who has treated a very inexperienced writer with unfailing patience and good humour.

MICHAEL FROST

Introduction

The fishing smack *Boadicea* first came into my keeping in February 1938. The change of hands was arranged during a chance meeting of no more than five minutes and no one was more surprised than I was. Without any designing on my part I suddenly became the owner of perhaps the loveliest of all the fishing smacks.

Even now I would think that there was no easy explanation of the matter, but at the time I had no doubts that there was some kind of fate in it. To put it another way, most owners choose their vessel, but from the outset I have always had a belief that in my case it was I who was entrusted with the care of the *Boadicea*. This of course had a profound effect on all my subsequent dealings with her.

Quite apart from that consideration, however, I still had every reason to be pleased at the way things had gone since she was exactly the shape and size of boat I wanted. She was also fresh from an extensive refit and in good condition throughout. Finally she was reputed to be the oldest smack afloat and this appealed to me strongly. During the years which followed I tried to find out her history and, in company with Hervey, with whom I had first learned how to sail smacks, I made a number of visits to nearby fishing villages trying to find some clue to her origins. None of these attempts was successful, but eventually, in late 1951, Hervey telephoned to me one afternoon and told me with excitement that he was in Maldon Custom House searching the records for something else, and had by chance come across the *Boadicea*'s original registration. She had been built at Maldon by Williamson and had been first registered in June 1808. The entry ran until 1825 when she had been sold to John Pewter of Tollesbury, who had re-registered her at Colchester.

We easily followed up this lead and found the 1825 entry in the Colchester register which continued until 1839 when Pewter wrote to say he had strengthened and partly rebuilt the hull, which was accordingly remeasured and re-registered in another volume which is not now at Colchester. Despite several inquiries I have not since been able to trace its whereabouts.

Not long after this, Hervey discovered that the granddaughter of one of the smack's previous owners was on his staff. She told him that her grandfather was still alive and, given the chance, would happily praise the *Boadicea* all day and every day. She suggested that Hervey and I should go to Tollesbury one evening to meet him. His name was Isaiah Binks and he was just on eighty-five, still very active though recently handicapped by failing eyesight.

It was arranged that we should go to Tollesbury on the coming Friday evening and, curious to know more about Mr Binks, I asked some of the older Mersea fishermen what they remembered of him. They could recall him as a past foreman of the Tollesbury and West Mersea Oyster Company, and told me that he had been a good one and a severe disciplinarian, which had led to the other fishermen calling him 'Manlaw' Binks.

I gathered that he had notably strong views about how fishing smacks should be sailed and worked and was outspokenly critical of crews who did not conform to his ideas. He was reputed to miss nothing and I was assured that, if I had deviated from his ideas about how the *Boadicea* should be sailed, he would certainly know about it and would not hesitate to put me to rights. I began to look forward to the coming interview with at least the beginnings of trepidation.

When the Friday came we went to Tollesbury to visit Mr Binks. His granddaughter answered the door to us and laughingly said that she was glad we had come in good time. Mr Binks had been fidgeting for the last hour and more. She led us through to a cheerful-looking room where the old gentleman was sitting waiting and introduced us. He rose to make us welcome and then almost at once began talking about the *Boadicea*. He was a strongly-built man with a rather round face and a short, very white beard. In appearance he could easily have passed for seventy and was vigorously alert in manner. He had a very determined way of speaking.

To my relief he made no criticism of the way I sailed the smack, but instead began by saying that until his eyesight failed him it had been one of his pleasures to walk down the seawall at weekends to watch the smack coming in. He took it for granted that I had already discovered for myself all the virtues of the smack and chiefly wished to meet me to tell me something of her history.

He told us that his father had become owner of her on the death of John Pewter. At the time he had been about six years old and could clearly recall the occasion. A neighbour had come to the door one evening and left a message that Pewter was dead and if Binks wanted the smack he had best go and speak for her without delay. His father changed and went forthwith.

He could just recall Pewter as a rather fierce old man, and since the two families were related, he had grown up conversant with the tales told about him. Pewter entered the Preventive Service as a young man and, when it was suspected that sunken contraband was being moored in the Wallet for later dredging up by local boats, he had been put on board the *Boadicea* with instructions to keep her dredging in the area. The Excise cutter had then sailed into Colne to leave the coast clear.

The ruse was successful and from the *Boadicea*'s decks Pewter watched while a number of local smacks dredged up their haul of dutiable goods and it was afterwards held that the identification of the vessels concerned led to the whole organization being uncovered and apprehended. Pewter was commended for his part in the matter, but was himself more taken up with the attractions of the *Boadicea*. He came ashore saying that no other boat could now please him and was determined that when she next came on the market he would buy her to work himself.

After this episode and, presumably for his own protection,

3

he was sent to do guard duty at St Helena where he remained until the death of Napoleon. When he came back to England he continued in the Preventive Service for the time being, but was still determined to buy the *Boadicea* when she next came up for sale. Eventually she did come on the market in 1825. He bought her at once and obtained his release from the service.

For the rest of his life he continued to work her and never changed his views about her excellence. It was his open belief that there was no other smack to equal her and he sailed her with the avowed intention of proving her superiority. He was a successful fisherman and, during his period of ownership stinted her for nothing.

Mr Binks told us that his father had been attracted by the *Boadicea* as a young man and had never wavered from his intention of succeeding Pewter in owning her. He too had sailed her with the avowed belief that she was the loveliest and most capable of all the smacks, and had acquired a reputation for good seamanship similar to that previously enjoyed by Pewter himself.

Towards the end of his life his father had given the smack a new keel and kelson, together with a complete new set of frames. The hull had then been replanked throughout. The old planking had been lapped, but the new skin was carvel-planked with caulked seams, and he, Isaiah, thought that the change had not improved the hull. The water did not flow as smoothly past the new skin as it had done with the old one and, although the change had made the vessel stronger, it had also made her pitch more in a seaway, so that she became heavier and rather wetter. She had never been quite as fast with the new skin.

He himself had taken over from his father and had worked her until he was made Company foreman and then, rather than see her lie idle, he had parted with her to Mr French at Mersea from whose son she had passed into my hands.

During the telling of this tale he was too much carried away to remain seated and instead paced up and down beside the table which he thumped from time to time to drive his points home. Towards the end of the story, however, he began to tire and, as he finished, his granddaughter guided him back towards his chair. He sat down again and, in easier mood, began to talk about the way a smack should be rigged and why the lead of the ropes and halyards had been arranged in the way it was. He was quite sure that the traditional layout was a perfection which would never be improved upon. This was a view I could easily accept and I was able to tell him that the *Boadicea*'s rig was still correct.

He then briefly outlined the method of using the gaff-cutter rig, but during this part of the conversation he was talking beyond the limits of my knowledge. Rather than interrupt I tried to remember his words as best I could and let the matter go at that. Later, by dint of much thinking and experiment, I probably did succeed in working out most of what he tried to tell me.

He moved on to more general topics and asked if she still had the small golden chariot at her mast-head which she had always boasted. I was able to assure him that it was still there. He told us that while at Tollesbury she had never had tar put on her above her waterline but instead the coal-barge had each year delivered from London a special gallon can of paint for her together with a yard of scarlet bunting for her streamer. He said that she had always been a very lovely boat.

He did not add to this and for a few minutes the room was silent. He seemed to be far away and was smiling to himself as though at some pleasant recollection. After a few more moments his granddaughter nodded to us and we rose to take our leave. He said goodnight to us almost absent-mindedly and we slipped quietly away.

While he was talking his manner had been urgent and there was no mistaking his wish that we should hear him carefully and not forget his words. Listening to him and sensing something of what he was trying to convey, it would have been difficult not to feel respect for him. Outside the house, in the rough weather of the January evening, we both still felt subdued and during the drive home neither of us made much attempt at conversation.

Even now, after the lapse of nearly twenty years the sense

and the message of his words are still fresh and, sometimes while sailing the smack at night, I have tried to conjure up a picture of him in his younger days nursing her through a seaway and have found pleasure doing so. His own father he had not described at all, but the almost legendary Pewter had been a rather fierce old man. How had he sailed the smack? From there it is not a long step to begin wondering what it is about the *Boadicea* which has caught the imagination of men so unlikely to be easily held captive.

Chapter 1

As a smack the *Boadicea* is so small as to be almost diminutive. She draws a mere four feet six inches which allows her freedom to work almost anywhere in the shoal water of the Blackwater estuary. Overall she is thirty feet long and this modest length allows her to work with room to spare in the narrow creeks. It also gives her a thirty-foot rig and, taken together with her other measurements, which are a beam of ten feet three inches and a displacement of just on eleven tons, this plays a large part in deciding the character of the vessel. For that reason it is worth understanding what the term implies.

For reasons to do with the need for easy reefing and the need for being able to heave-to steadily, the boom length of a working vessel cannot much exceed two thirds of her length plus say four feet of after overhang. This gives the *Boadicea* a boom length of twenty-four feet, which is ridiculously small, but any increase on it would make her virtually unworkable.

Boom length decides all the other dimensions of the gaff-

7

cutter rig. Thus the length of the mast from the hounds to the deck is the same as the length of the boom, while the gaff and the bowsprit are both about three-quarters of this length.

Balance and symmetry dictate that these proportions cannot be far departed from, and it follows that a long, lean cutter sets larger sails than a shorter, beamy one of the same tonnage. Against this is the fact that the more full-bodied hull of the shorter boat can carry sail better in hard winds.

Most of the smacks with which the *Boadicea* sailed and worked fell into one or other of two classes. A class of small thirty-foot smacks had a length and rig very similar to hers, but on average these boats had a displacement of only six or seven tons and were thus very much smaller smacks than she. The larger class had an average length of thirty-six feet and a displacement of twelve tons which was only a little heavier than the *Boadicea*'s eleven tons though their larger thirty-six foot rig was very much more heavy.

Had the *Boadicea* been less fortunate, this contrast between her tonnage and her rig might well have made her inefficient but, by good chance or perhaps by virtue of some genius in her builder, she seems able to combine the best of both qualities and, as need arises, draws on either her smallness or her bigness according to which is the more desirable. At sea she behaves as a heavy seagoing vessel, but in the close quarters of the creeks she is precise and as easy as a dinghy.

Seen out of water her lines are impressive and, looking at her, one can hardly help but be torn between respect for the artistry of the man who designed her and an admiration for the fortitude of the concept. Seen when afloat and lying to her anchor she is unobtrusive but, when sailing, and particularly when sailing in hard winds, she joyfully sheds this modesty and combines gracefulness with zest and verve.

As far as I know none of her previous owners has left any record of how he sailed her and during my own period of apprenticeship I have often regretted this because the records could have been authentic in a way which is no longer possible. These previous owners learned to sail while the art of seamanship was still being taught in a competitive school. At any time they had around them a hundred or more smacks all being sailed well and all vying and striving for superiority, but that era has passed away and, although during my own early years the art of sailing and working fishing vessels was still a living one, it had died out before I had done much more than begin to learn it. From there on I was able to increase my knowledge only by trial and error aided to some extent by memory. I would not claim to have mastered the subject though I had far better opportunities for learning than will be possible for any future owner, and since I know of no other source of information I have tried to set down as best I can how I learned to sail her.

In doing this I have tried to bring out technical matters in a day to day narrative of what my friends and I thought, and what we did, and hope that by adopting this method the story may catch some of the fun we found in living it.

Taken in this way the story cannot be separated from the character and geography of the coast on which it took place, and this of course unfolded to me as the range of my activities increased.

At the beginning I saw no further than the coastline of Mersea itself and if this had remained unchanged there would be no need to describe it, but in fact it has changed so much that it would be difficult now to recognize it as the same place. For this reason a brief description of what Mersea foreshore was like may be helpful.

Mersea is an oval island five miles long lying to the north of the Blackwater and separated from the mainland to the west and north by the creeks which drain the Virley, Peldon and Langenhoe marshes. To the east the end of the island is close to the deep-water channel of the Colne, but to the south a wide expanse of mudflats and shoal water separates the shore from the main channel of the Blackwater.

The mudflats are widest towards the east where low-water mark lies nearly a mile offshore, but towards the west the flats narrow until at the end of the island they are not much more than a hundred yards across. The offshore edge is scalloped by the running out of two watersheds which divide the length of the flats into three parts of about equal length. The watershed on the west runs in from the Sandbar as a narrow ridge of shingle and divides West Flats from Middle Flats, while to the east a similar ridge runs in from Cocum Hills to divide Middle from East Flats. West Flats were more or less firm to walk on but Middle and East Flats were treacherous and difficult to cross.

Until 1929 the greater part of the flats was covered by beds of *Zostera* or eel-grass, but during that year these beds died out quite suddenly. At low water the eel-grass lay as a thick mat on the mud, but as the tide rose the fathom-long blades of the grass were buoyant and floated to the surface. The grass beds thus formed a resilient but effective barrier to the action of the sea and I have been told that even in the roughest weather the smacks could find shelter by going no more than a few yards inside the edge of the eel-grass.

The eel-grass not only broke the force of the sea, but also obstructed the flow of water as the tide covered the flats on the flood and then drained away on the ebb. This resulted in the forming of clearcut outfalls in which the scour of the tide maintained breaches through the grass beds.

Each of the flats had a single outfall which had its beginnings as a shallow rill running close in along the shore but then turned out at right angles to run directly to low-water mark cutting a wide swathe through the grass beds.

Behind the grass beds where the shore was sheltered no sand was carried in but inshore of each of the three outfalls the run of the sea gave rise to a small beach which extended westwards from its point of origin.

Of the three outfalls the eastern one lay at the extreme range of my explorations and I never knew very much about it. As far as I can recall, it had no navigable value but the middle outfall was easily navigable and gave access to the barge quay below East Mersea church. The west outfall lay close in against West Mersea beach and, although not regularly used in my day, I have been told that in the past it was used not uncommonly by smacks taking the ebb out to sea since it carried eddy tide during the last hour of the flood.

Today the eddy tide still sets ebb-wise down the beach during the last hour of the flood, but the high mudflats off-shore have gone, together with the low cliff and greensward, which used to top the beach. The extent of the changes which have taken place can best be indicated by trying to trace out how they happened.

While the eel-grass was still there the mud on the flats was of two kinds. Flanking the outfalls it rose as smooth banks of soft grey ooze but, at the top of these banks where the grass beds began, the mud on the plateau surface of the flats was firmer and less regular. The grass beds were very much like sunken saltings, and most people supposed that the flats were areas of old saltings in the throes of being washed away.

Only when the grass had gone did the rapid erosion which followed make it clear that the grass had held the mud and was quite possibly the cause of it having settled there in the first place. Fifteen years after the grass had gone, a four or five feet depth of mud had washed away in the low water area and, as the underlying shale began to be exposed, it could be seen to carry lines of broken stakes clearly out-lining fish weirs of presumably mediaeval origin and oddly, among the stakes were the roots of trees with an average bole width of about five feet. At the time I first noticed this I deduced that both the eel-grass and the high mudflats had not appeared until after mediaeval times.

When the eel-grass and the high mud had gone the coast inshore of the flats was no longer sheltered and the beaches began to grow. In addition, the greenswards topping them began to be eroded to reveal that the turf had been growing not on salting clay as I had supposed but on the sand of some higher and older beach. This I construed as meaning that the greenswards had not grown until the eel-grass appeared to give shelter to a previously exposed area.

Both of the watersheds still persist to show that the tidal currents remain in the same directions as before, but with the going of the high mud the outfalls no longer carried enough scour to maintain themselves and in the general erosion all three have disappeared.

Apart from the need to treat the watershed areas with caution, a smack could now sail at high water almost anywhere across the flats with water enough for safety, but while the grass was still there this was not so and navigation over the flats was more or less confined to the deeper water of the outfalls which for part of their courses lay close in beside the shore.

It was my good fortune that at high tide the deeper water lay close beside Mersea beach and my interest in fishing smacks began when one of them used this channel. As I assess it now her skipper was showing his companion that the shelter of the grass beds could be used to win a mile of easting before the ebb set down in the main tideway. By chance I was able to watch this lesson and something about it caught my imagination.

Chapter 2

It is difficult to be sure how old I was when I first began to be taken to West Mersea beach, but certainly by the time I was seven I knew the whole length of the greensward fairly well, and was already allowed out on West Flats when the tide was out, though Middle and East Flats were strictly forbidden.

At first my interests were not nautical at all. I was more attracted by the wasteland that lay behind the beach. Later on I struck up friendship with a Mersea boy and the pair of us began going out over the mud to help gather winkles for the fishermen who worked on the eel-grass beds.

The motives behind this were not wholly creditable as we soon found out that by the time the winkle brigs had enough water to work their way in over the flats to load the filled sacks there was too much depth in the outfall for us to wade ashore. Sometimes the fishermen would send us back to the beach in good time, but if we did manage to stay on the flats late they had no alternative but to pick up the pair of us and take us with them in the brig along with the sacks of winkles. On her way home the brig would then put us ashore on the King's Hard. This was a path laid across the flats at the west end of the beach and from there we would make our own way back to where we belonged.

These short sails in the winkle brigs roused my interest and I began to pay more attention to the smacks which could be seen distantly working in the river. They were too far away to be seen very clearly, however, and it was one of my disappointments that when one of them did appear from behind the island she did not obligingly come closer, but instead held away outside the flats drawing steadily further out to sea. Each time that one did appear I hoped against hope that this one would keep close in. Eventually one of them did so.

The incident occurred just before high water on a cold rough day with the wind blowing hard on shore. The tide was a big one with the water rising well up the cliff which topped the beach so that it was almost level with the greensward itself.

Offshore from where I stood the water was grey and windswept, but fairly smooth as the eel-grass out on the flats was breaking the force of the sea. Further to the east where the outfall turned away offshore there was much more swell, and the surf was breaking continuously over the greensward edge.

When the smack first came in sight she was coming out of Bussand under three reefs with a reefed staysail, and at her bowsprit end she was carrying a very small storm jib. This combination of sails gave her the open-rigged appearance typical of fishing smacks in gale conditions, and even from a distance she looked exciting. From the moment she began to bear away to come inshore I felt certain that this smack would indeed sail past me so close that I could almost touch her.

Close reefs can be set in different ways but smacks, which are heavily ballasted and low in the water, very often set their sails high even when reefed. At sea this gives the vessel more drive, but not the least of the reasons for doing it is the far better appearance of a vessel when she is slightly high-reefed.

This smack had her reefs set high and as she swept in to cross the King's Hard fairly well inshore she was sailing fast with her bow-wave rising up round her rail though she was not heeling very much.

As the smack approached she was still drawing in closer to the shore until eventually, when she had fairly reached the beginning of the outfall, she was not much more than her own length distant from the greensward edge. She then held along the shore at about this distance out and quickly drew towards the place where I was standing.

I surmise now that she was almost certainly one of the smaller smacks, but at the time she seemed enormously big and strong. This impressed me, as also did the stormy appearance of her bow-wave, but surprisingly the noise of her going through the water was far less than the shrill noise of the wind in her rigging. Perhaps most of all I was impressed by the appearance of ease and safety of the men on board of her. Before she was fully past me her bow-wave swept in and topped the cliff, but I hardly noticed this in the excitement of waving and shouting to her crew. There were two men on board, one of them, young and fresh-faced, was sitting on the rail just aft of the rigging. This one waved and laughed but the second man who was half-crouching at the helm was older and severe-looking, and paid no attention to my shouting. This did not surprise me as even in the little winkle brigs I had learned that the helmsman is remotely un-approachable. I watched him glance from ahead to aloft and then to seaward and then aloft again – the glance aloft was long and searching.

After the smack had passed she continued close in for a short distance, but then began to ease away gradually from the shore, so that by the time she reached the rougher water to the east she was fairly well out. I watched the younger man move aft and begin hauling in the mainsheet. He hauled quickly, hand over fist, with the rope snaking out behind him to the deck and I could easily imagine the weight and the pull of the smack's mainsail. As the sail came in the smack headed away more offshore and came close up on the wind. She was clear of the sheltering grass beds now and

I watched the first sea of the rougher water break round her bows.

I had not seen anything like this before and for a moment was anxious, but before the thought had barely time to form the younger man moved over and took the place of the skipper at the helm. The old man moved across to weather and then for a few moments stood looking aft as though weighing up and judging the passage he had just completed.

The act was simple but its meaning was clear enough. The passage down the length of the beach had indeed been skipper's work but now, forging her way out to the Sandbar end and the open sea beyond, the smack needed no more than a boy to manage her. My fears dispersed and were followed by a relief and a faith in fishing smacks which no other kind of vessel since has ever stolen.

On my return home that evening I described the incident to my father and found him an understanding listener. He agreed with my belief in the great seaworthiness of fishing smacks, and told me that from the nature of their work they needed to be capable of staying at sea working while other boats sought shelter. He told me that a boat of similar build to the one I had been describing had been sailed single-handed round the world. This had been done by an experienced seaman to whom long passages were commonplace, but it was remarkable that he had been able to show that such a small vessel could be perfectly at ease in all kinds of weather with only the minimum of attention.

Shortly afterwards he bought me a copy of Slocum's *Sailing Alone Around the World* and during the evenings read it to me. When the book was finished he gave me another, this time Bullen's *Cruise of the Cachalot*, with its similar message of a vessel being comfortable at sea in spite of the storms and adventures which took place round her. I enjoyed both books and easily understood them and thus, by the time I was just on nine, and had made no longer voyage than the length of West Flats in a laden winkle brig, I had no doubt at all that to be seaworthy a vessel must be at ease with the sea and must be able to look after herself with only the minimum of tending. I was quite sure that these qualities could be found in their highest perfection in working fishing boats.

Some time later I was taken down to Mersea Hard to look at the long lines of fishing smacks brought-up in the creeks, but they were too far away to see very clearly and did not make very much impression on me. My clearest recollection of the day is of an abandoned smack lying close in to the saltings beside the Fisherman's Hard, and this smack I determined was the one I would one day rebuild and take to sea. Alas, before very long she was broken up and only her keel remained, as it still does to this day, though recently the beach has extended further to the west and now has covered it.

Chapter 3

The breaking up of the smack by the Fishermen's Hard seemed to me to be wantonly destructive, but before I had very long to grieve about it I was put to a new school and for some years my interests were taken up in other directions. I never fully forgot the fishing smacks however, and some eight years later when I had left school and was a student travelling daily by train to London, I quite often drew fishing smacks on the misted carriage windows.

On one such occasion I was sharing a carriage with a school-friend and he commented on the smack I had drawn. He had not before known I was interested in boats and wondered whether I would care to join a syndicate he was forming with the idea of hiring a boat at Rowhedge. He told me that joining would cost me five shillings each week. The intention was to sail each Friday evening and come back on the Sunday at whatever time the tide served.

This idea appealed to me at once and before we reached the end of the journey the arrangement was completed. I paid my five shillings and agreed to meet him and a com-

panion at the mud dock which lay at the far end of Rowhedge waterfront. I was to bring a blanket and some food
and, if possible, an oilskin and a pair of seaboots. If I was
going to buy these, the Army and Navy Stores was the best
place. The name of the boat was the *Beryl*. She was painted
white and I would find her very easily.

When the Friday came I took the evening bus to Rowhedge
and had no trouble finding the boat, but I was the first one
down and did not go on board until the others came. The
Beryl was freshly painted and still had her lifeboat sheer line.
She had a good foredeck and a low cabin-top inside narrow
side decks. Aft of the cabin was a fair-sized cockpit and
behind that was a small after deck. She was sloop rigged with
a short bowsprit and her mainsail sheeted to an iron horse
behind the cockpit. Her sails and spars were bright and to
my eyes looked very nautical.

I sat on the grass bank beside the dock and studied her
gear and rigging and, by the time Alan and Geoffrey arrived,
had worked out what each of the various ropes did, though
I was none too sure of the names of them.

We went on board and unpacked our things and then at
high water poled the *Beryl* out of the dock on the ebb tide.
There was no wind and since none of us had any idea of
how to sail her we agreed that there was no point in making
experiments in full view of the Rowhedge and Wivenhoe
veterans.

We simply let the *Beryl* drift down river at her own speed
and, by the time the last light was going, we had reached a
point just short of Alresford Creek. Here we dropped
anchor and put out a riding light. We then retired below for
our first seagoing meal and our first night afloat.

As far as I can recall the syndicate never had a skipper.
We had all been at school together and were all easy-going.
Our decisions were arrived at after much discussion, but
since none of our opinions was likely to be right we seldom
had firm views about them and never seriously disagreed.
Later the syndicate had a fourth member, Tom, who knew
rather more about it.

On that first evening we were all a bit dubious about how we would ever get the *Beryl* back to her mud dock again but next morning, when we undid the sail tiers and set up sail, we fairly easily found out how to persuade the little sloop to go in the direction we desired.

The first weekend was a great success and for the rest of the summer we regularly left Rowhedge each Friday. We made no very long passages and on the whole were fairly sensible, though we did sometimes try to make the little life-boat turn to windward in weather which was too rough for her. We soon discovered that under these conditions she was difficult in stays, and in rough water quite often had to gybe her round. We accepted this as a matter of course and did not regard it as being a defect on her part. On the contrary, we were convinced that by definition a lifeboat is a good seaboat.

This was as it should be, but sometimes when we chanced to sail in company with one or other of the two Rowhedge smacks which shared our mud dock with us, all my old long-ings for fishing smacks returned and I could not conceal from myself that as seaboats the smacks had a solidly purposeful way with them which no yacht could aspire to.

Towards the end of the summer the *Beryl*'s owner told us that for the next season he would be needing the boat him-self and, in addition, Geoffrey had been warned at work that he would soon be shifted to another area. Regretfully we tried to get used to the idea of the syndicate dissolving.

Coming back from the last sail of the season, we drifted up Colne listening to the sound of Wivenhoe bells silvery-noted in the distance, and we all felt that we must make one more attempt to save the situation.

We tidied up the boat on the way and when we reached the dock put all our gear on shore. We then took the key back to the owner and made one last attempt to plead with him. He was quite firm however and we could not perusade him to change his mind. We handed the key over and sorrowfully made our way back to the dock to collect up our things.

After the *Beryl* syndicate had dissolved I found that being confined to the shore for weekends was now too dull to be accepted easily, and began trying to arrange a berth for myself on board one of the two Rowhedge smacks. This was difficult however as neither of them worked to any regular hours and seldom, if ever, fished on Sundays. There was in fact a strong feeling against fishing on Sundays.

Failing in that direction I continued to make inquiries, and eventually a schoolfriend sent me to Lewis Worsp at Wivenhoe, whose firm employed two smacks at that time. Here again I found the same trouble about irregular times of going out and the avoidance of fishing on Sundays, but rather than disappoint me altogether Mr Worsp arranged to go out for a Saturday pleasure trawling himself and invited my friend and I to join the party. He would take the *Prima Donna* out on the following Saturday and we could join at about ten o'clock at Wivenhoe Quay.

The *Prima Donna* was the smaller of the firm's two sailing smacks and had a Harwich bawley-type hull, though she was cutter-rigged in the same way as the Colne smacks. I joined her on the Saturday as arranged and we took the ebb down. This was the first time I had been on board a fishing smack while she was sailing, and the experience was every bit as good as I had imagined. The wind was fresh south-westerly and under a single reef the smack sailed fast but felt tremendously safe and steady. We crossed the Colne Bar by the inside swatch and then pulled down a second reef in preparation for trawling. Setting the trawl was too complicated for me to follow fully, though the main principles were clear enough and I was able to help without being too much in the way. When the net was over and fishing I took up position leaning in the weather rigging in the way I had watched and so much envied in the past. I found it was a comfortable and very satisfying vantage point.

On our first haul we made a good catch and decided to sail back to make the same haul over again. While the others cleared the net I was given the helm, and sailed the *Prima Donna* under her two reefs in fairly rough water and found it wildly exciting. Not only was the smack solidly satisfying to sail, but equally satisfying was the knowledge that in the whole hull and rig there was nothing gimcrack, and nothing make-believe. The smack was a real one and she felt it.

In due course we reached the Bar and I was told to come about ready for trawling, and then we lounged again while the hove-to smack towed her trawl away down-tide to leeward. This time however the haul was not uneventful and after a short time the smack stopped quite suddenly, with her warps stretched out bar-tight to weather while the tide sluiced fiercely past. Vaguely I followed the proceedings while the other two took the after warp forward and let the smack swing head to tide. This brought her through the wind's eye and, sailing herself on the other tack, she dragged the net free. For a few minutes we were busy hauling the trawl back on board.

I gathered that the net had fouled some kind of sunken obstruction, a situation known as 'getting fast', and also that we had been lucky in coming clear so easily. Although the net was upside down when we hauled it back on board it seemed to be undamaged and we cleared it and then put it over again. A neighbouring smack meanwhile sailed over and asked us for the 'marks' of the fast, but we had to confess that we had not taken them. The smack luffed away but from the expression on her skipper's face I gathered that we were badly in disgrace.

This was above my head, though I did realize that marks were simply transits which fix the position of the obstruction. Even so I could not imagine how anyone could have been taking transits in the moment of trying to get a fouled net clear of an obstruction. Not until twenty years later did I find out that while trawling a good fisherman is watching his marks all the time so that at any moment a mere glance will tell him exactly where he is.

On the *Prima Donna* that day I am afraid to say that we did not bother with transits at all, but we made an excellent catch of fish, and by evening time had all that we could use. We came in at dusk, and since there was not yet enough water to get up to Wivenhoe we went into Pyefleet to lie the night there.

This was another new pleasure. The weather had been rough all day, but as darkness came the wind increased and at high water the *Prima Donna* was sheering back and forth heavily. From below, where we were roasting before the cabin fire I listened to the harsh snubbing each time she reached the end of a sheer, and then the moment or two of almost unnatural silence followed by the sturdy slap of water round her bows as she paid away again. The timing of the various sounds fascinated me and the quality of them was as different again from the lightweight behaviour I had grown used to in the little *Beryl*.

During the evening while the other two yarned I was content to lie back and listen while I studied the *Prima Donna's* heavy oak frames and deckbeams lit and shadowed in the firelight. The method of her construction was so simple and yet so obviously strong that I found myself concluding that sound principles are always simple and only cleverness confuses them.

In the morning we sailed back to Wivenhoe and, after tidying the smack in readiness for her regular crew to take over again on the Monday, we came ashore at the turn of the tide and parted company. I took a goodly string of fish home with me, but much more important came back fully confirmed in my beliefs about the virtues of fishing smacks. I was of course tremendously excited about the whole business and that night, for the only time in my life, I sleepwalked. In answer to an urgent summons to come on deck I climbed out of my bedroom window and broke a wrist in the fall which followed. This was serious as it might lead to me being forbidden to make any further smack expeditions and after climbing back I lay low for the night wondering how to avoid that disaster.

In the morning I found that I also had a very fair black eye, but to my relief the family seemed to take the matter in its stride, and apart from packing me off to have my arm attended to made no further comment though my friends took a great delight in the black eye for which many reasons were invented.

Chapter 4

The *Prima Donna* trip was never repeated and, during the period when I was mooding about on shore waiting for my arm to get better, I spent a good deal of time looking round to find a small boat which I could afford to buy. I was attracted by a winkle brig with a cabin which was lying at Rowhedge and had a notice in her rigging to the effect that she was for sale for eighteen pounds, but the problem was where to find that amount of money.

I was sure that my father had none to spare, so there was no chance of scrounging it, but it did seem to me that just possibly I might be able to save enough from my pocket-money. I set out to try this, but after about two months of starvation I had saved only six pounds and in the meantime the winkle brig was sold. I decided to try building a boat out of income.

Having reached this decision I put the plan in hand and bought myself a good stem, and a length of three-inch elm to make the keel and stern-post. I then bought a baulk of silver spruce which I had sawn into wide boards to make the planking. This ran me out of funds for the time being and inquiries showed me that a piece of wood wide enough to make the transom was likely to be impossibly expensive. This led me to scrap the idea of having a transom. It would be much cheaper, and just as good to make the boat a double-ender.

I had no previous knowledge of boat design, but worked out a rough system from first principles. My only real guide was a determination that the boat to be seaworthy must be fairly short, very wide and have a nearly flat floor. I drew out my lines on graph paper and then transferred the sections full-size to my bedroom floor where they looked just as convincing as any other set of lines. At that time I did not realize that boats' lines all have this misleading quality.

Using the bedroom floor interfered with the ordinary cleaning of the house and caused some criticism although I had used only a black chinagraph pencil on the polished wood. My father came to hear of the matter and wished to be shown the lines. He studied them critically for a few minutes and then to my surprise said he would make me a present of a square of floor boarding which I could use to make the moulds. He would ask for two longish planks to be included and from them I could make the battens. Needless to say I was very grateful for this unexpected windfall, but I was also aware that I was now committed in good earnest and would have to do my work well and properly.

I had often helped my father with his own spare-time carpentry, and was familiar with tools though by no means expert at using them. I set about making the moulds carefully and found that they were not difficult. Within a short time I had them all made and then set up the hull on its stocks in a spare part of a barn beside the house. When all the moulds were standing and the battens on, the assembly looked almost professional.

The next problem was to make a pattern for the two garboard strakes and, not being able to think of any better way of doing it, I pasted together thickness after thickness of paper until I had made a semi-rigid paper garboard for one side. This took the evenings of about a fortnight to complete,

25

but it did its job well when finished and with suitable cutting and trimming the same length of paper served as a pattern for all the other planks on the hull, so the work involved in first making it was not out of proportion.

To my relief I found that the planks cut to the shape of the paper pattern fitted the hull without trouble, and they bent round into place much more easily than I expected. In fact, during the planking up my only real anxiety was the tremendously full body I had so gaily designed for the hull. However, as more planks were added the shape began to look more reasonable.

In addition I was of course becoming used to looking at the new creation and I have no doubt that this played its part in soothing my anxieties. Either way, plank followed plank and I bought myself a second baulk of the silver spruce which gave me enough wood to finish all but the two sheer-strakes. This took me the whole summer to do, but at least I was not bored and was agog with ideas about how the hull would sail and handle in a seaway.

For the sheerstrakes I decided to use Honduras mahogany which could not be obtained in Colchester and for this I made a special journey to Maldon. I had read all sorts of tales about lesser kinds of mahogany rotting away and was on tenterhooks lest I should be sold some substitute material.

Sadds's foreman sawyer was a kindly man and when I sought reassurance from him he stooped beneath the saw and picked up a handful of sawdust. He asked me to smell it and then told me that no one on earth would use a wood which smelt like that unless it had some quality which other woods did not possess. This was a convincing argument. When the planks were cut he swept all the dust away from them and went over both with me carefully. He was very matter of fact and asked me to say whether or not I accepted them. I said that I did, and he made me out a chit of paper which he told me to take to the office. I could leave the wood with him and it would be delivered during the next week. He then cautioned me to cut the sheerstrakes very carefully. Whatever I did I was not to cut into the grain, always to cut out of it. He asked me if I knew what he meant and I easily said yes because I had already discovered this hazard while cutting the silver spruce. He told me the mahogany was far less to be trusted than the spruce and on no account to hurry while making the cuts. He also told me to leave it under wet sacks for a couple of days after it was cut and to bend it very slowly.

When he had finished giving me all these warnings I thanked him and took my chit of paper to the office to have the wood priced. When I received the bill I quizzed it as it was a good deal less than I expected, but the clerk assured me it was right so I paid it and came home feeling that I had been let down very lightly. In fact I think I had over-estimated the cost of the wood and the bill was all right, but even so I still recall my sawyer friend with affection and, incidentally, he was the only master-sawyer I have met who wore gold earrings and a blue seaman's sweater.

The wood arrived as promised and very carefully I cut out the two planks. The sawyer's warnings were well-founded, and repeatedly the offcuts started away in long shakes, but the planks themselves came out without blemish. I soaked them for a week before bending them and they went round without trouble.

Boat-building was not my only occupation however, and I was at least in part conforming to student ideas about sport. During the winter I played football fairly regularly and in the summer spent about the same amount of time playing golf. It was golf which led me into one of my more foolish expeditions on the mudflats off East Mersea.

For some reason a golfing friend and I decided to hire a sailing boat from West Mersea and go down to have a look at the golf course just inside the seawall at East Mersea. We hired a boat called the *Colne* from Sidney Hewes who kept the shop at the top of West Mersea causeway and sailed down to East without trouble, but on the way back found that we were not making headway and while keeping in out of the tide ran the boat ashore off East Mersea church. It was evening by now and we decided that, to pass the time until the boat floated, we would wade in across the flats and have a meal in the East Mersea inn.

The eel-grass had been gone for about five years and a good deal of the soft mud had already washed away, so the wading was not too difficult, but even allowing for that the decision was not sensible.

With daylight to help us we were able to pick our way over the firmest part of the flats easily and reached the beach still fairly clean. We wiped the mud from our legs and plimsolls and set off to walk up to the Dog and Pheasant where we had a meal and then spent half an hour lounging in the bar. It was dark by now and after a bit we set off on our way back to the boat in what we thought was fairly good time. Without hurrying we made our way down the lane to the beach and then started out to recross the flats. We had no doubt at all about our sense of direction, and not for a moment did we suppose that the boat might be difficult to find.

It had not occurred to us that the going would be more difficult in darkness than it had been in daylight, but we quickly found out that it was, and by the time we reached the edge of the incoming tide we were already muddy and out of breath. To our surprise there was no sign of the boat at all, but we still did not doubt our sense of direction. We supposed that since we had taken longer crossing the flats than we had meant to the boat was by now already afloat, but we thought it would still be within wading distance, and with almost unbelievable folly began wading out in the direction in which we confidently thought she must lie.

For quite a long way we made good progress, but then struck a patch of lumpy mud over which we were slowed by numerous rills and pot-holes into which we fell without warning. Before very long we were both wet through and it soon became obvious that we would be lucky if we found the boat.

With belated good sense we decided to turn back and make our way ashore. The tide was now flooding strongly, but we could still distantly see the uncovered part of the flats inshore from us and we began the return crossing without anxiety. The pot-holes were slowing us however, and the tide was running in faster than we were. Very soon the flats inshore were no longer visible and we now realized that the evening was misty. No lights could be seen either from the shore or from the lit buoys out in the estuary. There were no stars and there was no wind.

Our only guide was the flow of the water round our feet, but I knew that although the first flow is directly in towards the land, this direction changes as the flats cover, and the changes are not at all predictable even when one knows one's position relative to the watersheds. When the watersheds cover, the whole area is confused with turbulence until there is enough depth for the main eddies to develop. Only for a short period would the run of the tide continue to give us help and we had no time to waste.

We carried on for about twenty minutes, but my friend was flagging badly and we stopped to let him get his breath back. He now told me that he had a weak heart and was not allowed to make strenuous exertions. This was an unexpected complication and the situation began to look much more serious.

His chief trouble was falling each time we stumbled into one of the pot-holes. The lumpy mud was slippery and not easy to cross at the best of times, but now that it was covered so that we kept falling into holes unexpectedly it was almost impossible to avoid making strenuous efforts to keep one's balance. In the deeper holes the water was up to our shoulders. They were too narrow to swim across, but most of them had firmish floors and once into them the actual crossing was not too difficult. If we could solve the falling in and the climbing out we might still be all right.

Until now we had been moving side by side, but we thought it might make it less strain for him if I went ahead so that he could pause when I fell in and I could then steady him while he slid down. He could wade across by himself, but on the far side I could climb out of the hole first and then pull him up. This seemed a reasonable scheme. We tried it and for a time it worked well and we were making good progress, but it was still too much for him. After a while he stopped and said that he could not go any further. He would wait until he had got his breath back, and then try to make it swimming all the way. He suggested that the most sensible thing to do would be for me to go on ahead and find the beach, after which I could guide him by hailing and he was sure he could swim the distance fairly easily.

This was plausible but I altogether distrusted the idea. We tried to argue the thing out logically but were at cross purposes. For a time we stood silent and obstinate. Oddly enough we were both unwilling to try swimming until there was enough depth of water to carry us over the tops of the lumpy mud.

In all we stood for about five minutes, and then both together we heard faintly and far away a sound which was unmistakably the soft rustle of shingle as a small wave broke on it. The sound was repeated and then again. The direction was off to one side from the one we had been making but it was quite clear. Beyond doubt the sound was coming from the beach and this changed everything. Heart or no heart, my friend now agreed to make a series of short moves and at each pause we were able to listen and check our sense of direction. With the urgency now gone we had no need to hurry unduly, but by the time we did reach the shore the water was well up round our waists which was quite deep enough and we were not at all sorry to wade out to the security of dry land.

Quickly we stripped off and combined forces to wring our clothes out as dry as possible. We then set out to walk back down the island to where we had left his car at the top of West Mersea Hard. We soon became warm again, but were still damp when we reached the car. He offered to run me back to the top of the lane beside East Mersea church, but there was no point in doing this as it would be six hours at least before I could get back on board again. I would be far warmer walking than waiting idle on the beach. He agreed to drive straight home to have a hot bath and go to bed.

Even at that I was worried about him as I made my way back along the foreshore, and hoped he would not suffer any lasting ill-effects from the night's activities.

I arrived back well before daylight and the tide still had another two or three feet to ebb before the flats would begin to uncover. With several hours wait ahead of me I tucked myself into a crevice in the cliff with the idea of trying to keep as warm as possible.

Now that I had nothing else to worry about I began to be anxious because we had not intended the *Colne* to lie to her anchor for the whole tide and had foolishly shortened in her anchor cable by about half. I felt sure she must have picked up her anchor at high water and visualized her by now drifting miles and miles down the coast. With that thought to distract me the last hour waiting for the dawn was quite the worst part of the whole night. However, when daylight did come the *Colne* was still riding where we had left her and looked secure enough, but I was surprised to see just how far out from the shore she was and the full extent of our folly of the evening before began to be apparent to me.

As the flats uncovered I wondered whether to begin wading out early, but decided that I would get myself warm first by going for a brisk walk along the beach, and even when the boat came adry I still delayed wading out to her as I guessed that it would be some long time before she would float again. The sun was gaining strength by now and although still chilly the weather was fine. By the time I did start out over the flats it was a clear, crisp autumn morning. I reached the boat easily and, as the water was still some distance off, lay down on the floor-boards and was warm enough. By about nine o'clock the water returned and not long after that the *Colne* floated and swung to her anchor.

I gave her about ten minutes more and then set up sail and hauled the anchor on board. There was almost no wind, and the water was crystal clear. As the tide drifted the boat over the uneven surface of the flats I lay in the sun and watched over the side and could appreciate why we had found such troubles the night before. Later in the morning a light easterly breeze sprang up and I was able to sail out into the deeper water, and then square away to run back to Deeps. More by luck than judgement I correctly chose Mersea Fleet from the various entrances ahead of me, and as the *Colne* made her way up towards the causeway I saw Charlie Hewes begin walking down. I guessed he would bring a dinghy off to the *Colne*'s mooring and went to it direct and brought up fairly capably.

A moment later he came alongside with an amiable grin and I was relieved as I had been more than half expecting a rebuke. His first comment was the casual statement, 'See you've bin a'wading, Mick', and I agreed that I had, but did not explain the full extent of our foolishness of the night before. He told me that he had walked down to the beach at dusk, and had seen the boat anchored on the edge of the flats, and had taken it that we were all right. In the morning he had noticed that the car was gone and had guessed roughly what had happened. He looked at my clothes and told me I'd been lucky, from which I gathered that he knew enough about the flats to work out for himself what we had been doing. He put me ashore after helping me to tidy up and stow the sails and refused any thought of paying for the extra time we had the boat out.

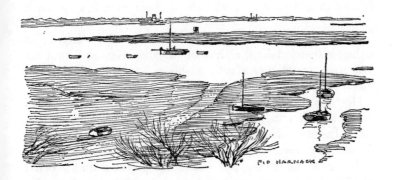

Chapter 5

After the escapade on the mudflats I carried on with the boatbuilding. The sheerstrakes were finished and the next step was to make the frames. For these I decided to use rock-elm and this again was unobtainable in Colchester so I made another trip to Maldon.

I wished to have the frames as thick as possible, but not thicker than one inch, which would have been difficult to bend properly.

I sought the advice of my sawyer friend and explained the problem to him, but before making any decision he questioned me about how I had made out with the Honduras mahogany. I gathered that he had been mooding about my choice of this wood ever since and had concluded that as far as durability was concerned I would have done better using oak. However he was relieved that I had been able to cut the planks out and bend them without making a mess of them.

He agreed with my choice of rock-elm for the frames and thought that at one inch thick I would have no trouble bending them. It was important, however, that I should have a narrow wooden steam-box as my supply of steam would be limited. On no account was I to try using a metal pipe as a steam-box as this would take all the heat even if I lagged it well.

He sorted out some elm sap-wood and cut four lengths six inches wide to make the sides of my steam-box and told me that they would cost almost nothing. I took his advice and added them to my order.

He then sorted through a pile of rock-elm planks an inch thick, and selecting several with clean straight grain cut me thirty frames twelve feet long and an inch and a half wide. When they were cut he went over each of them carefully with me before asking if I would accept them and, when I said I would, he gave me my chit to take off to the office. The bill was again very reasonable and I paid it as a well-satisfied customer.

In due course the wood was delivered and I made up my steam-box, but there was now a problem because I intended to use the hull itself as the template for bending the frames and I was forbidden to have any kind of fire near the wooden barn in which the hull had been planked up.

A trial attempt showed me that I could easily steam the frames enough to make them pliable, but once out of the box they cooled quickly. There was no alternative but to shift the hull outside well away from the barn and this was done without mishap. With the help of two friends I began the steaming early on a Saturday morning and by the evening of the Sunday had more than half of the frames bent into place and lightly fastened top and bottom. The rest we completed during the following weekend.

This part of the work was exciting but the next part, which was drilling the holes for the fastenings, was slow work and not in the least exciting. As a first move I drilled and countersunk all the holes and placed the copper nails in them, but set the roves only on those frames next to the moulds. Even at that I made slow progress and it was full spring before I was able to take out the last of the moulds and see what the

34

vessel would look like when she was finished. In fact she looked very well.

After the moulds were out I took a weekend off and with a friend arranged to hire the *Colne* for a Sunday and go out sailing. In the event the day was a rough one and as we stood at the top of Mersea hard the noise of the wind in the telephone wires was not comforting. My chief anxiety was about money and I was worried about the possibility of doing damage to a hired boat and then not being able to pay for it. Charlie Hewes brushed this aside and said that provided we stayed in the creeks the boat could not come to very much harm. Accordingly we set off and found that closely reefed the *Colne* behaved very well. During the afternoon we explored Salcot and Virley creeks and went for a short sail outside in the river, but it was too rough and we decided to come in. Against a strong spring ebb the *Colne* would not make up to windward in Mersea Fleet and eventually I decided to take the sails down and row. In fact the *Colne* did not row very well and against wind and tide we made slow progress. Several people I knew passed us in their dinghies and I took a good deal of ragging for not being able to sail the boat in properly. Eventually we did get back to the causeway and with relief handed the *Colne* over without having broken or damaged anything. What we did not know was that somewhere outside my elder brother and a friend had capsized their dinghy without anyone knowing it had happened.

In fact both of them were lost, but I was sheltered from full knowledge of what had happened and to this day do not know the details. For some time my father continued to hope that they had been picked up by a passing freighter and would be landed in due course at some distant port, but as this hope faded with each day that passed he became visibly aged. Working on the boat I was building was obviously out of the question and, when not in London, I spent my spare time on the golf course.

After about two months my father drew me to one side and told me that it was not fitting that I should give up the building. I should take up my tools again in good faith and carry on where I had left off. He was not a man to be argued with and certainly not on that occasion. Very unhappily I did as I was told, but wished heartily that I could find something less obtrusive than the horribly noisy riveting.

The noise I was making did not seem to upset anyone unduly, and I carried on until evening. When I did finish and came indoors it seemed to me that the atmosphere in the house was if anything more relaxed, and on the Sunday I carried on again without any great worries.

That was one thing, but it was quite another when a day or two later one of my friends asked me if I would care to spend a weekend with him crewing on his boat at Mersea.

He had in fact been one of the people who had ragged me while we were rowing the *Colne* up Mersea Fleet and I at once realized that the invitation had been made with a full knowledge of the background. Not knowing what to do I accepted tentatively subject to what my parents had to say about it.

Whether or not I had any real intention of asking my father I cannot now remember, but in the event I did so, fully expecting him to endorse my own view that going was out of the question. In fact, he thanked me formally for having sought his advice and told me that both he and my mother had already decided that I was to lead a normal existence and not to be influenced by any anxieties on their behalf. He added that the sooner I went out sailing again and came back safely the better it would be for the whole family.

I accepted that he really meant this, but was too young to assess the good sense of his statement fully, and on the following Saturday evening went off still feeling very unhappy about the whole business.

I met Peter on the causeway, and together we went off to the *Bonito* as his boat was called. After stowing our gear we put a kettle on and then sat yarning. Although I had been at school with him we did not know each other more than casually, but he was easy-going and good company, so that by the time the tea was brewed we were discussing boats and sailing with my anxieties more or less forgotten. We turned in late, but were up early next morning, and after a good breakfast got the *Bonito* under way and had a pleasant enough sail but came in fairly early. On returning to the mooring we stowed the sails and to my relief packed up our things and went ashore fairly quickly. Peter ran me back to Colchester in his car and dropped me off at home soon after tea-time. My parents were curious about where we had been, and how the *Bonito* had sailed, and after discussing the sail over a meal I spent the rest of the evening catching up with some of my studying.

As far as I could work it out my father had been quite right and the household had now returned more or less to normal, and certainly as far as I was concerned I slept better that night than I had done since the day of the accident.

During the week I met Peter again, and he asked me if I would care to crew again for the coming weekend, and this time I accepted without hesitation. He told me there was no need for me to wait until he could get down in the evening. I could go down during the day and if I wished to I could take the dinghy out to pass the time. This I accepted delightedly and went home to tell my parents without any qualms.

My father suggested that if I did take the dinghy out it might be worthwhile going up to Ray Island which he had always found a pleasant anchorage. If I did go to the Ray he would like me to look for a well he had dug there many years before. In his day fresh water had been something of a problem and he had dug the well on Ray as an experiment. At about seven feet he had found water which was slightly brackish but easily drinkable. His other sources of water had been St Peter's Spring near West Mersea church and a spring on East Mersea bowling green which he had boxed in. I had seen these last two, but had not before heard about the well on Ray, and began to look forward to trying to find it.

On the Saturday I set out early and caught the bus to West Mersea. This took me as far as the church and from there I would make my way on foot to the hard. I had two alternative routes. The first was a folly which led inland direct between the main village and the fishing hamlet by the hard, while the second was the somewhat longer walk round Coast Road. This was the more interesting of the two and was the one I chose.

At first Coast Road leads between rather dull walls and houses, but soon reaches the open shore, and then for a few hundred yards runs along on high ground overlooking the creeks and the main Blackwater estuary. When I had reached about half way along this high part of the road I paused and for a time leaned on the iron railing while I studied the lie of the creeks and checked that I was clear about my geography.

On the seaward side of the road the ground dropped away in a steep bank and immediately below was an area of turf and reeds which I knew was called Hove Marsh. On the village side this was bounded by a garden wall which ended close against the foreshore, and at its lower end the wall was topped by a roofed vantage point known to all and sundry as 'the monkey-house'. Beside the wall a track led down from the road to the foreshore, and quite close to this was a freshwater outfall called St Peter's Spring. From there Hove Marsh stretched away to the west for a few hundred yards, and at the far end was bounded by Hove Creek which drained the marsh and in its lower part ran from beside the road straight out towards the mudflats offshore.

Close against the road Hove Creek led through a hove or culvert over which a path ran out to the marsh but then forked to form two paths, one leading to the monkey-house and the beach beyond, while the other ran beside the creek and led down to the Fishermen's Hard.

The fishermen claimed rights over the whole of Hove Marsh which they said had been given to them by a queen long ago when they had sailed over to help the men of Kent, but which queen this was and how long ago I have never been able to discover.

Offshore from Hove Marsh the beach petered out just to the west of the monkey-house and from here only a bare salting edge separated the marsh from the mudflats. At this point West Flats have narrowed down to become a mere strip of mud lying between the foreshore and Bussand Creek.

Looking at the mud I could see the irregular contours of the old 'lumpy mud' where the grass beds had been and these extended almost up to the Fishermen's Hard.

The Fishermen's Hard is artificial. A shingle path leads down over the mud to a made-up shingle patch at low-water mark. It is a very old hard, however, and I would suppose dates at least from the days when the rights over Hove Marsh were granted to the fishermen.

Bussand Creek is usually spelt 'Besom' on the charts, but this I have always believed to be the perpetuation of an error made by the earliest cartographers and I have never heard a native Mersea-man call the creek anything but 'Buzzen', which I take to be a corruption of Bussand in the same way that 'Rayzen' is a corruption of Raysand. In dialect 'Besom' would be pronounced as 'Bayzum'.

Offshore from Hove Marsh Bussand is more or less straight, and runs south-east along the edge of West Flats towards its mouth well down in front of Mersea Beach. It is in fact the only one of the creeks to have its own mouth out to sea. To the west of Hove Marsh the creek follows round the end of Mersea changing its direction towards the north.

On its offshore side Bussand is bounded by Cobmarsh, a roundish salting island about half a mile from east to west and rather less across. To the east Cobmarsh runs out to seaward in a long spit of mud known as the No'thern, while to the north-west a shorter mudspit called Cob Spit separates Bussand from Mersea Fleet. Cob Spit is bare mud, but the No'thern, in common with most of the seaward spits in the estuary, carries a fair-sized hill of broken shell. Locally these hills are called shram-hills, and their shape is quite distinctive. Some are formed on the ebb and others on the flood, but the up-tide end is always a shallow fan of shell spread out on the surface of the mud while the down-tide end is a high bank with steep-to sides. Since the eel-grass had gone the shram-hills had tended to move further down tide.

Beyond Cobmarsh lies Mersea Fleet, and inland where Cob Spit peters out Bussand and Mersea Fleet join to become one, but while Mersea Fleet is open at low water the inshore end of Bussand comes adry.

On the far side of Mersea Fleet is Packing Marsh, a narrow salting island lying at the seaward end of a long mudspit called Middle Ooze. Both the marsh and the mudspit lie more or less north and south. Packing Marsh is owned by the Tollesbury and West Mersea Oyster Fishery Company and carries two oyster packing sheds which give it its name.

Packing Marsh and Middle Ooze separate Mersea Fleet from Thornfleet which is the main deep water channel into Mersea. The two creeks are parallel and run more or less north and south. On its far side Thornfleet is bounded by Feldy Marshes which end in a point just opposite the sheds on Packing Marsh and on the far side of this again lies Copt Hall Creek running in from the north-west to join Thornfleet. Locally, Copt Hall Creek is almost always referred to as 'Ditch', or sometimes 'Little Ditch', and in dialect the vowel is pronounced long as in 'eye'. Beyond Ditch, is another salting island called either Sunken, or sometimes Half-sunk Island and beyond this again is Salcot Creek.

The seaward ends of Packing Marsh and Sunken Island are of about the same length so that Mersea Fleet, Thornfleet, Ditch and Salcot Creek join here to form a single expanse of deep water known as the Mouth of Deeps.

The Mouth of Deeps runs south-east and is sheltered between Cobmarsh and the No'thern to the north, and Old Hall Marsh to the west. Further to seaward Old Hall Marshes end, and here Tollesbury Fleet runs in from the west. The combined channel is now called Deeps.

Even Deeps is fairly sheltered because outside, and lying between it and the main Blackwater estuary the mile-long spit of the Nass runs out from Shingle Head on the Tollesbury shore. In dialect Nass is pronounced with the vowel long as in the word 'car'. The spit carries a shram-hill similar to the one on the No'thern but a good deal longer and higher. From Coast Road the beacon marking the end of the Nass can be seen bearing about south-east, and standing apparently well out in the river. Inshore from the beacon, but somewhat to the east of it the spit of the Nor'hern ends and Bussand joins the main estuary.

Satisfied that I was able to pick out and name each of the

six main creeks which lie at the west end of Mersea I then relaxed to enjoy the picture that they made. As seen from Coast Road they are laid out as a vista which according to the weather may be bleakly cold and grey, or if the sun be shining is traced out as an intricate lacework of green and silver. On that morning the green had the quality of emerald while here and there the brown sails of oyster skiffs showing above the saltings lent an added touch of colour and served also to remind me that here since beyond Roman times the cultivation of the sea has been more important than farming of the land.

I pondered all this and decided that there was virtue in a form of cultivation which could be so pleasantly unobtrusive, and enjoyed the fact that the only person in sight was an elderly fisherman walking up the path from the Fishermen's Hard with an oyster tendel on his hip.

I watched him reach the culvert of Hove Creek, where he stepped down to the pool of water and carefully washed his seaboots. With that done he waded the creek and made his way up the slope to reach the road. He began walking up Hove Hill towards me and rousing myself I picked up my things to resume my own walk to the hard. We looked at each other as we passed but made no greeting.

Later I was to know that this was William Mussett from the fishing smack *Ida* which had her mooring in Bussand. Morning after morning I used to pass him at about the same place and same time, and then one day I wished him good morning. To my surprise he stopped and talked to me. I had by then come to regard him as being the doyen of the Mersea fishermen, which he probably was, and, full of curiosity, I asked him what sort of catch he had in his tendel. He lifted the piece of clean, wet sackcloth inside it and showed me that the basket held about a dozen soles, all beautifully cleaned and skinned. I commented on the large size of them and he told me that he kept only the choicest of the fish he caught. He added drily that small fish grow into big ones if they have the chance. I quizzed him as to why he was always home so early and he laughed quietly. One had to fish early to fish alone, but he went on to say that it was no use fishing on to catch more than could be sold for a fair price. This conversation was several years later but on that first morning I was aware of an instinctive respect for him.

Reaching the bottom of Hove Hill I was now down to the level of the foreshore, which from Hove Creek continued on as an expanse of open saltings dug out to form mud-berths, some of which were occupied by house-boats. From here the road began tending more towards the north, and after a few hundred yards the strip of saltings ended abruptly in a dock and quay opposite a newish brick-built public house called the Victory.

Beyond the dock, the fringe of saltings began again but was now narrower and was dug out to form a system of oyster pits with paths and drainage rills between them. From the Victory to the hard was only a few hundred yards more and on the landward side of the road the rough bank of sloe bushes began to give way to the garden fences of cottages which stood back partly out of sight. This was the beginning of 'the city', a fishing hamlet said to have been named from a public house of bygone days but probably both names were a corruption of something older. The hard formed the western end of the island and was a natural outcrop of shingle which extended down from a strip of greensward by the road to the bed of the creek below. About three hundred yards from end to end, it was bounded at this southern end by a slipway belonging to the shipwright firm of Clarke and Carter, while at the far end a small quay known as the No'the had been the starting point of the carrier to Colchester and perhaps long ago to Rome. At the middle of the hard a causeway ran down nearly to low water mark and about midway between this and the No'the a second slipway belonged to the shipwright firm of Wyatt's.

The vista, which from Hove Hill had been one of marshland threaded through by creeks, had now changed, and with the rising tide covering the mud-spits the hard was faced by a wide stretch of open water.

Bussand had joined with Mersea Fleet to form a single creek loosely called 'Fleet', though this name was also used for Mersea Fleet itself. Either way, Fleet skirted the hard and beyond it lay the Middle Ooze, now covering with water. Beyond that again lay the deep channel of Thornfleet bounded on the far side by Feldy Marshes. Fleet and Thornfleet did not join but continuing side by side were connected by a narrow cross-channel called the Gut. About fifty yards long, this lay opposite Wyatt's slipway and carried two or three feet of water at low tide. The Gut which ebbed into Thornfleet and flooded from it, was a kind of boundary because to the north of it both Fleet and Thornfleet changed their names.

North of the Gut, Fleet continued as Strood Channel curving away to the east to join up with Pyefleet and the Colne to separate Mersea from the mainland, while Thornfleet continued as Ray Creek which also tended away slightly to the east and ran inland as far as Peldon.

Ray Creek and the Strood were separated by a tongue of marshes which ran out from Peldon and ended at Ray Point opposite the No'the. Running down from the point Ray Spit formed the north shore of the Gut and was of firmer mud than the Middle Ooze on the other side.

Ray Island which I intended to explore was a gravel outcrop about half way down the length of Peldon Marshes and had a different character from the other islands. Cobmarsh, Packing Marsh and Sunken Island were true islands in a sense, but they covered on the big tides and were bare of all but salting vegetation. In contrast, Ray Island was an island only while the big tides covered the surrounding saltings, but being above high-water mark it was true land and had trees and bushes growing on it. I could see the rounded clump of trees which marked its position, but I was none too sure about the best way of getting there.

On the way down from the church I had met only William Mussett, but here at the waterfront there was more activity and several people were in sight. Just short of Clarke and Carters a group of fishermen were packing bags of oysters ready for the carrier, and out on the hard two or three boats were being worked on. I carried on down to Sidney Hewes's shop which was set back behind a small garden facing the

43

causeway. The shop was to be my first port of call, and I put down my things on the grass verge beside the road.

Long ago Sidney had owned and fished a smack called the *Fiddle*, but nowadays he was fully occupied in running the shop and a fleet of hire-boats which he kept lying nearby to the causeway. The *Bonito*'s oars and rowlocks were kept at the back of Sid's, and custom dictated that anyone going round to the back while the shop was open, first went in at the front and bought at least a bar of chocolate. I decided that I would do this and ask Sid's advice as to how best to set out on my way to Ray.

In reply to my question Sid asked, 'Going exploring Mick?' and when I replied that I was he came out in front of the shop to give me directions. He began with the *Bonito* lying in the Gut. From there I was to carry on through the Gut and then turn away north up Ray Creek. After rowing about half a mile I would come to Sampson's Creek running off to the west. I was to pass that and about four hundred yards further on I would come to a gravel beach running down from the clump of trees which was the centre of Ray Island.

If I decided to go exploring on the saltings towards Peldon I was to watch the tide as the path from the mainland was worn down and covered some time before the saltings did and was then difficult to find in the maze of creeks and rills. He checked that I understood my directions which I did, though his Essex dialect was so broad that it was by no means easy to follow all he said. I thanked him and went round to the back where I easily found the oars and rowlocks. Returning to the front I went down the causeway and found the dinghy which I launched down.

The *Beryl* had never possessed a dinghy and this first occasion on which I launched a dinghy down was in some ways a milestone. A dinghy of my own would have been delightful no doubt, but it would also have been inescapably a toy, and almost by definition not the real thing. Vaguely I debated this as I rowed off. I was certainly not yet graduated to the status of mate on the *Bonito* and decided that at best I could regard myself as a visitor invited for the second week-end in succession. Even so, everything has to begin somewhere and I was very much on my best behaviour. Using a dinghy was a new science and I had better learn to manage it properly in a seamanlike kind of way.

The *Bonito* was tidy and shipshape as we had left her on the previous weekend, and I stayed only a few moments before setting off up Ray. With the flood tide in my favour and the wind behind me I made good speed and easily found Ray Beach. I landed there and hauled the boat up so that I could put the anchor well above high-water mark.

My exploration of the island did not produce any great finds. The north-western part where the well had been was overgrown with brambles, and the dead wood beneath the bushes was so dense that I eventually gave up my search without having found any trace of it. Inshore from the bramble patch I found a low circular rampart. This was partly grown over with stunted hawthorn bushes which I guessed as being a hundred years old and probably more. Several of the bushes carried old nests which from their heavy build I took to have been made by sparrow hawks, as they seemed too low to belong to herons but I did not see any of the birds.

Outside the area of stunted trees the island was covered with rough grazing and was of rounded outline towards Peldon but on the Ray Point side it tapered away parallel with the salting edges. I made a circuit of high-water mark without finding very much and then came back to a hummock overlooking the marshes towards Langenhoe and Peldon. Here I sat down to laze in the sun and eat my bar of chocolate.

The tide had made quickly and the saltings were beginning to cover. Within a few minutes the island was surrounded by a wide expanse of sunlit water. Apart from the slight noise of the wind in the trees behind me there was no sound other than a lark which I eventually spotted very high up and slightly to the south of me. Idly I pondered the contours of the distant mainland. Directly inshore from me were Peldon heights which ran eastward towards Langenhoe where the ground dropped away to the Colne valley, and then further away through the haze I could see the high ground of Alresford and Thorrington on the far side of the Colne. Between me and the Colne lay the wide area of marshes separating Mersea and the mainland. I decided that before the Colne had taken a short cut out to sea between East Mersea and Brightlingsea it had almost certainly flowed behind Mersea to have its mouth this side of the island, but why the little gravel hill of the Ray had formed I was unable to work out.

The tide rose and made its mark and then began to ebb away. While the saltings were still covered there would be no easy finding of Ray Creek, and I was chary of getting the dinghy aground and stranded somewhere in the middle of the marsh. I decided to wait and continued to lie in the sun until mid-afternoon, when the water had ebbed away clear. I then roused up and returned to the beach where I boarded the dinghy and set out to go back to the *Bonito*. On the way down Ray I made a short detour to explore Sampson's Creek which is walled across just inside its entrance. Finding nothing of note there I did not delay further as I was beginning to feel thirsty.

I reached the *Bonito* uneventfully and went aboard looking forward to making myself a brew of tea. When this was made I took it out to the cockpit to drink at leisure while I sat in the sun and watched the people who were beginning to come off to other boats in the creek.

After a time a tall youth in a frayed blue guernsey came alongside in his dinghy and passed the time of day. Almost dozing I had not noticed him approaching, and for a few moments I could not place him but then realized that I had seen him in the distance the weekend before. I recalled that his name was Hervey and that he was the owner of a small black cutter with tanned sails. I returned his greeting, and he asked me amiably how I had got on with my exploring. Surprised because it had not occurred to me that my activities would be of interest to anybody else I told him that I had made a tour of Ray Island without finding very much and had then looked into Sampson's Creek on my way back. It had been a rather uneventful day but a very satisfying one.

This seemed to amuse him in a good-humoured way, and

he told me that he too had spent many hours exploring the creeks and saltings with just as much pleasure and enjoyment. For a time we yarned, and then he said that he must be getting back on board to tidy up before his mate Frank came down. He told me that Frank would be coming down in Peter's car so that we should probably see each other again when we both went ashore to meet them. He pointed out to me his boat which was lying further down Thornfleet just short of Packing Marsh and told me that she was called *Kestrel*. With that he pushed his dinghy clear and began to scull away down Thornfleet.

I watched this with interest as I had not yet learned how to scull a boat. Without any obvious effort and without rolling the boat appreciably, he fish-tailed the oar back and forth over the dinghy's stern and made good speed through the water. His wrist was making a figure of eight movement as he guided the loom of the oar and the same surface of the oar blade was uppermost on both port and starboard strokes. I decided then and there that when Peter came down I would ask him if I could cut a sculling notch in the stern of the *Bonito*'s dinghy, as it was obvious that I must learn to scull as soon as possible.

In the evening I met Hervey again when I went over to the causeway, and we spent several minutes in conversation until Peter and Frank arrived. After some further talking while we loaded their gear into the dinghies we separated and each crew rowed off to their own boat.

On the Sunday evening we all met again when we came ashore. There was some discussion as to whether Peter and Frank could get away early on the following Saurday as it would be the August weekend and Hervey wished to go further afield than the usual weekend cruise. However the pair of them had arranged already to go to a party on the way down so that idea fell through. It was agreed that Hervey and I should meet them at the causeway at about ten o'clock on the Saturday evening.

On the August Saturday I again went down early and set off in the dinghy. The tide was ebbing and the day was fine with a light southerly breeze. I decided to take the ebb down

Bussand and explore Cob Island. I would then continue down and come back round the point of the No'thern. This went uneventfully and I made a short tour of the saltings of Cob Island then carried on down Bussand. The shram-hill was just coming adry so I stopped to make a tour of that too. I found that it was similar to Shell Island which lay on the offshore edge of West Flats, though very much larger, and with a greater variety of whole shells round its base. The in-shore end was the steep one and lay about a hundred yards short of the Cob saltings. By the time I had studied the lay of the shram-hill the tide had ebbed well away down the No'thern and, after rounding the point, I had a longish row back up Deeps, but stopped on the way to examine a hill of shingle on the edge of the mud. The hill was made up of relatively large stones and I could not account for it ever having formed, but was later told that it was a ballast heap dating back from the days when trading brigs had unloaded ballast before picking up a freight. Reaching the mouth of Deeps I decided to come back by way of Thornfleet and arrived at the *Bonito* by about low-water time. On the way I passed the *Kestrel,* but saw no sign of Hervey.

In the evening I went ashore and found Hervey already waiting but no sign of the other two. We had a long wait together and variously yarned and discussed my explorations of the day. Peter and Frank were late, but did arrive eventually and seemed to have enjoyed their party very well. We ragged them about this and then before parting company arranged that the two yachts should rendezvous in Deeps at tide time next morning to sail down to Colne in company.

In the morning we met as planned and, after a little adjustment of the sails, found that we were able to keep the two boats sailing at the same speed very close together. The conversation between the two crews was light-hearted and chiefly concerned the party of the night before. Watching the *Kestrel*'s straight stem cleaving the water only a foot or two away I began to feel depressed. She looked so very much like a miniature fishing smack that all my old longings came back to me, and I felt irritable and out of place sitting in a yacht's cockpit discussing parties.

I knew very well that I was lucky not to be spending the weekend killing time on a golf course, but this did nothing to improve my spirits. I longed for a boat that would have a stem the same shape as the *Kestrel*'s but heavier and stronger. A boat that would lift and drive in good earnest. Gloomily I decided that yachts were toys and could never hope to be the real thing. I wanted a boat that was genuinely committed to the sea for reasons that were adequate. Well aware that I was being ungrateful I kept my thoughts to myself without being very happy in them.

We sailed up Colne as far as the Geedons, and then came back to bring up just inside Brightlingsea Creek. In the evening we all went ashore together to explore the saltings on the St Osyth side and we carried on along the shore until it was almost dark. On the way back I dropped behind to look at some wreckage half buried in the sand, and when I caught up with the others again I found that they were discussing the pros and cons of swapping mates.

Apart from the fact that Frank was a much more experienced crew than I was this seemed a fair enough suggestion, and would fit in with our various times of finishing work before the weekend much better than the present pairing. Frank had no objections, and with visions of being mate on a miniature fishing smack I certainly had none. The new arrangement was agreed to and, when we returned on board, Frank and I gathered up our belongings and changed berths.

As I climbed over the *Bonito*'s rail into the *Kestrel*'s boat I could hardly do other than recall my longings of the morning and wondered vaguely about the speed at which things happened. Later in the evening, after we had turned in Hervey was reading and I lay in my bunk looking at the *Kestrel*'s deck beams set on a proper smack-style shelf and was reminded of the *Prima Donna*. It seemed to me that I had reached at least half way towards the kind of realness I was seeking. Eventually I got off to sleep but was too excited and was full of dreams.

Chapter 6

Next morning I was awake early and crept out to examine my new charge. It was a very lovely morning and the *Kestrel* lived up to my expectations. While I was still examining the lead of her halyards I was surprised to hear Hervey saying 'good morning', and turned to find his head half-turned towards me while he himself was jammed awkwardly in the hatchway.

He was amused at my advance reconnaissance and came out to explain anything I found difficult. After I had been round all her halyards and sheets we went below again and had breakfast. We then did the cleaning up between us. He said we would not wait for the *Bonito*, but would get away while there was still plenty of water.

This we did in a light easterly breeze and wended under the *Bonito*'s stern before bearing away to run down to the entrance of the creek. I tidied up the halyards and anchor and then went aft to rejoin Hervey in the cockpit. He pointed out the buoy at the end of the spit which I must leave to port and then giving the helm to me disappeared below. A few moments later he put his head out again and said that he had some reading he must catch up with. He passed a chart out to me and told me the lead-line was in the locker at my feet. As an afterthought he added that it might be wise to keep outside the Bench Head Buoy on the way back. He then disappeared again. For the next three hours I heard no more from him and blithely supposed that perhaps he might be sleeping.

I had sailed the *Colne* single-handed back from East Flats without making much fuss about it, but then I had been a free-lance. This new responsibility was different. At any time the skipper might come out and ask where I was, how much water I had and what course I was steering. Without realizing it I had slipped into the habit of sailing 'by committee' rather than taking it that the helmsman is responsible. I began to realize that, although I had passed the Bench Head Buoy many times I had only a vague idea of where it was and, disconcertingly, the morning was hazy. I settled down to navigate in good earnest.

That was good training, but I had another preoccupation. On no account did I wish to do anything which might bring the skipper out on deck, so my navigation was all done furtively. In due course I did find the buoy, but only after passing through a noisy little tide-rip which had two fathoms of water under it. I then schemed out how I could gybe round the buoy without waking Hervey and succeeded in getting the sail over almost soundlessly. I paid the mainsheet out very gently, but to my intense disgust the gaff-jaws began to creak abominably and I felt sure that my period of single-handed navigation was now over. There was no sound from below however and I began to relax again. The *Kestrel* was only just making up over the ebb but I was in no hurry. Apart from the buoy dropping slowly astern there were no marks visible, but to starboard I had the edge of the shallows to use as a handrail and was confident that I could keep in touch with it.

Holding along the edge of the shallows I was gradually drawing in closer to the shore and eventually saw the huts on West Mersea Beach. Not long after this I heard sounds from below and Hervey put his head out. Without looking round he said that he supposed the Nass was in sight ahead and all well and I assured him that it was so. He had put a kettle on before coming out and I handed over to go below and prepare a meal.

We did not go straight in, but crossed the river and brought up under Bradwell beach, and for a time sat in the cockpit yarning. He told me that the *Kestrel*'s previous owner had sailed with Charlie Hewes as professional skipper, and drew me a vivid little word picture of Charlie cooking plum-duff in the formal little fo'c's'le and then serving it to the equally plump owner in the formal saloon. He surmised that both Charlie and the owner usually had second helpings. It was partly through Charlie that he had come to buy the *Kestrel*, and it was through Charlie's influence that the *Kestrel* had a mooring on the Company ground in Thornfleet.

The *Kestrel* herself was a neat little Victorian yacht with a straight keel and stem, and a very handsome rounded counter. She was cutter-rigged, with a longish bowsprit, and was slightly over-sparred and canvassed. I hardly admitted that she was so unsmack-like as to possess a cockpit, but in fact she did have one and it was quite in keeping with her.

Hervey already knew of my interest in fishing smacks and turned the conversation in that direction. He himself thought that barges were the last word in sailing craft and was openly amused at my refusal to admit them as potential rivals.

In the evening we got away again and returned to the mooring and, when I went below after scrubbing the decks, he told me that he had cleared a space for my gear in the fo'c's'le, and I could leave anything which I did not need to take ashore. I accepted with alacrity since this kind of privilege was usually won only after long apprenticeship. I realized that my new skipper had a very generous way of doing things.

The following weekend was a lull period and the only matter of note was that almost without ceasing we continued the smack versus barge argument. I think it ended in something like a draw, but when we parted on the Sunday evening he laughingly said that we could have the second instalment next week.

In the event it was not so. He met me at about six and we went down to Mersea in his car. During the journey he was quiet and I sensed that something was worrying him. Later while we were rowing off to the *Kestrel* he remarked that he had heard that Charlie Hewes had decided to sell the *Charlotte*. This was unexpected news, but whatever reply I made it was certainly non-committal. The *Charlotte* was Charlie Hewes's much-cherished fishing smack.

For the rest of the weekend the subject of smacks was avoided, but although we did not talk of them we were both thinking, and possibly our thoughts were running parallel, because apropos of nothing he said that there was no possibility of buying the *Charlotte* unless he sold the *Kestrel* first. This was thoroughly upsetting and I asked him to put the thought out of his mind. It was inevitable that I would one day own a fishing smack, but that did not mean that everyone else had to do the same. He was very fond of the *Kestrel* and should stick to her and in any case I loathed the whole idea of buying and selling boats.

He mooded about this for a few moments and then, going off on a different tack, said that there was nothing inherently wrong with buying and selling boats. I disagreed strongly. We dropped the subject and did not refer to it again.

Even so I was worried about the situation. I was quite sure that the *Charlotte* was not really on the open market, which amounted to supposing that the news would not have reached Hervey unless it had been meant to.

Charlie was the Oyster Company foreman. This was a highly prized position which carried responsibility for the whole area of beds fished by the Company. Few men would have refused the offer of the appointment which was accepted as going to the best of the senior oystermen, but it carried one big disadvantage. Whoever held it worked on the Company Foreman's smack, which meant that unless he had sons to carry on, his own smack was left lying idle. Charlie had no sons and was well aware that idleness is almost the worst enemy of a boat.

The *Charlotte* had been lying idle for a long time, but there had not before been any talk of selling her, in fact the reverse, and it was generally understood that he would never let anyone else sail her.

This was the background to the new information which, if it were true, meant that Charlie had changed his mind. I felt quite sure that this change of mind was only partial. He would let her go to Hervey if Hervey wanted her. It was a great compliment but it put Hervey in an awkward position, because he was very fond of the *Kestrel*.

We came back to the mooring fairly early on the Sunday evening and for a time lounged. When it began to grow dark we started clearing up the cabin ready to go ashore. We had nearly finished this when John Howard came alongside in his dinghy. He was the owner of a small winkle brig called the *Oxbird* and knew Hervey fairly well. He chatted for a few moments and then asked if he could come on board. We at once invited him to do so. He came below and we wondered what had brought him, as visiting on Sunday evenings was unusual. He seemed rather ill at ease and his manner was forced and unconvincing.

For a time the conversation was general and there seemed to be very little point in it. I was beginning to fidget and wonder when he would take himself off so that I could finish the tidying up when, without any leading up to it, he said that he had heard the *Kestrel* was for sale and he would very much like to have first offer. This was a bombshell and for a few moments no one spoke.

Finally, Hervey said that he had not really thought of selling her, but would at least consider a fair offer. This was not part of a mate's province and I wriggled back into the shadows while the two skippers negotiated and came to an agreement. It was not a final agreement because no one knew whether the *Charlotte* was really for sale, but subject to that the deal was more or less agreed on.

Not long afterwards he took his leave and Hervey made a comment about having his mind made up for him. I could sympathize but resisted the idea. He had a free hand to choose as he wished. We agreed on this, but then both of us had to admit that even beyond Charlie and his plans there was something of fate in the matter.

I had felt this while listening to the negotiations, and one part of my mind had been racing on ahead. There were a number of smack-yachts in Mersea, but these were smacks which had been converted into yachts. They had been dismantled and rerigged, and had all their working gear thrown out of them. Half their ballast had been taken out and sold, and as they lay at their moorings they looked unnaturally high-sided with the beginnings of their bilges showing naked at the waterline. They had been stripped of one pride and fobbed off with a lesser one to survive only as unseemly hybrids, neither one thing nor the other. I could easily see that Charlie would never willingly let this fate befall the *Charlotte* but, vaguely also, I could appreciate that by some quirk of chance the only two people I knew of who would not do this had just joined forces and were more or less available.

I could understand why Charlie had decided to change his mind and could see the method in his planning, and I listened to the negotiations agog with excitement at the prospect of being possibly the mate on a proper smack. True, she would be an amateur smack but that I could accept. Mate on a smack-yacht I never would be willingly. It was near enough a vow.

Chapter 7

Two weeks later the dealings were completed and Hervey had handed over the *Kestrel*. He left a message for me that he would not be able to get down until lateish on the Saturday, but had shifted both his gear and mine over to the *Charlotte*. He had arranged with Charlie that if possible I would be on board at midday when Charlie would bring out a new mainsail which he had in store. He would help me bend the new sail and would then take the old one off ashore with him.

On the Saturday I went down early and without delay rowed off to where the *Charlotte* was lying in Thornfleet just beyond the Packing Sheds. During the row out I could barely contain my impatience, but when I did reach the smack I found unexpectedly that I was almost unwilling to board her.

Standing beside her as the dinghy lay alongside, the *Charlotte* seemed to claim her privacy very strongly, and it occurred to me that just possibly the boys had been ragging me. The message about Charlie and the mainsail could have been a hoax.

I debated this and decided that almost certainly the message was genuine. Even so, I would have been happier to have had either Hervey or Charlie there to lend propriety to my boarding her. I wished I had waited to meet Charlie on the hard and he could then have brought me off himself. The message had been clear enough however, I was to be on board at midday and I had better stick to that.

Almost reluctantly I climbed on board and made the painter fast. I would wait until Charlie came off, but would stay on deck rather than intrude below. That seemed to be a fair compromise.

Once I was on board I felt much less out of place and enjoyed sitting on the rail studying the *Charlotte*'s halyards and noting where each of them belayed. Meantime, the creek was deserted and no one was in sight to question my right to be there.

After about half an hour the Company smacks came in and I saw that Charlie in the *Our Boys* was leading them. The *Our Boys* had her mooring about a hundred yards further inside the creek and was bound to pass fairly close alongside. Hoping very much that Charlie would not resent my being on board I waited to see what he would say as he did go past.

The *Our Boys* was carrying full sail and Charlie eased her in towards the *Charlotte* so that she passed no more than a foot away to leeward. She was a big smack and at close range made a very striking spectacle. Charlie waved to me and hailed cheerily. He would be coming off with the sail in about an hour's time. I hailed back and was relieved that he had not seemed at all upset.

Hard on the *Our Boys*' heels half a dozen other smacks swept past, and on each in turn the crews made all kinds of ragging comments. I was much happier now however and ragged back at them light-heartedly. While the smacks were bringing up I sat and watched them, more than slightly suspecting that a special exhibition was being staged for my benefit. Later, when the crews went off ashore I made a brief exploration of the *Charlotte*'s hold and cabin.

Towards midday I came on deck again. The *Charlotte* was

lying to the flood and was almost head to wind, so the changing of the sails was not likely to be a problem.

I could see the causeway from the smack and eventually saw Charlie coming down with the new sail on his shoulder. I watched him lower it carefully into his boat and then saw him push clear and begin his half-mile scull out to the *Charlotte*.

He sculled without effort but was making good speed over the tide and about ten minutes later eased his boat in alongside. As usual with him, he made no greeting and, after leaning over to take his painter which I made fast, I slipped into the boat with him. Together we lifted the sail over the smack's bulwarks and let it roll down to the deck.

We then both climbed on board and, while I let the boat go aft, he rummaged in his pockets, producing in turn a ball of spunyarn, a small coil of cod-line and his clasp-knife. These he laid on the cuddy-top. With a grin he told me that on the big yachts they were for ever changing mainsails and it was one of the first things the boys had to learn when they joined the smacks.

He did not add to this, but the words conjured up a picture of an eleven-year-old Charlie joining his father on the smack, and I wondered whether quite possibly he had been greeted with the words he had just used to me.

We set to work methodically and changed the sails fairly quickly. While doing this Charlie did not talk very much and I soon realized that he was saying only the things which he intended me to remember.

When setting up the old sail before freeing the mast-hoops, he made me haul both the throat and the peak halyards together and pointed out to me that, when hoisted in this way, the gaff rose horizontally. This was not just due to chance. The throat halyard had a three part purchase but the peak was four part and to make the gaff rise evenly the gaff strops for the peak halyard had to be in their right places.

He did not add to this, but his words conveyed the clear understanding that whether the sail was being raised or lowered, the *Charlotte* was not to be seen with her gaff any other than shipshape.

When the new sail had been hoisted, he walked fore and aft several times looking at the set of it from various angles. He then nodded his head as much as to say that it would pass. Having decided that, he turned his back on the sail and stood leaning in the rigging while he looked thoughtfully at the water over the side.

For a time he continued silent and then, without turning, began talking in a quiet, careful voice. Without any leading up to it he told me never to start the jib halyard while the sail is at the bowsprit end. Always when downing the sail to begin with the outhaul. This will bring the sail in to the stem-head where it will lie quietly until it is run down.

After a pause he went on to say that while wending, the jib sheet should never be let fly. Instead it should be eased out as the sail needs it, but checking it a little so that the sail crosses the forestay without much more than a ruffle in its surface. This I could easily understand. A vessel wending is a truly graceful thing if given half a chance to be so.

He paused for quite a long time and then began again. While sailing, the staysail should be kept on its bowline and when wending it should not be allowed to go over until it is ready to do so. When it does go, it should go once and then stay there without flogging on its horse. As soon as it is over it should be put on the bowline on the new side.

I was not to be afraid of overpeaking the mainsail and, if the vessel needed to be driven hard to windward, she needed to be overpeaked to get the best from her.

He told me never to let the boom drabble and I knew exactly what he meant. The after end of the boom should always be raised about ten degrees above the horizontal. As an afterthought he added that the bowsprit should never be so slack on the bob-stay that the outboard end bent upwards and that too I could understand.

If too much pressed, the smack could be quickly eased by letting the peak run, but never to ease her by starting the throat. A scandalized sail was no credit to anyone, quite apart from being nearly impossible to lower after it had been scandalized.

He continued silent for a bit and I guessed he was trying to think of all the unsightly things which people do to boats. Finally, he said always remember to start the clew outhaul when coming in to bring up, as otherwise the mast-hoops would jam and then come down with a run.

He turned round and grinned. He had shown me how to set the mainsail, now I could lower it and stow it single-handed. This was a tallish order for someone who had never done it before, but although I twice had to look to him for advice I did it reasonably well. When the stow was finished, he pointed out to me that the reef-points of the first reefs were hanging evenly beneath the sail.

We rolled up the old sail and lowered it into his boat. He then told me I could cast off and I did so, coiling the painter neatly in his boat's bows. For a moment he stood glancing up and down the length of Thornfleet, to make sure that all was well in his domain.

Without a word he pushed the boat clear and shipped his sculling oar. He swung the boat round and with no hint of farewell or any backward glance began sculling away towards the hard.

As he went, I leaned on the *Charlotte*'s boom and watched him, wondering what thoughts did go on inside his head. While waiting for him to come off I had been worried in case he should be sorrowful, and had supposed that the new main-sail was not just due to chance, but was rather the result of some long-thought-out plan and was his parting present to the *Charlotte*.

At any time he tended to be sparing with his words, and although his long silences never gave the impression of un-friendliness, I had been prepared for a glum and embarrassed time with him. In fact, he had been more talkative than usual and had seemed to enjoy the task of telling me how he hoped the smack would be sailed now that we had charge of her. I did not have any doubt at all that this was what he had been telling me.

Later on, I went ashore and picked up Hervey. With the ebb tide now half way gone, we wasted no time but set up sail and got away under jib and main. By a narrow margin we got the *Charlotte* round without putting her ashore and then relaxed as, rather majestically, she beat out towards Deeps. Once outside, we bore away and reached down to the Bench Head and then gybed to run into Colne. We brought up in the entrance to Pyefleet and after clearing up on deck went below to sort out the arrangements in the cabin.

Sailing her had been both satisfying and delightful. Her bulwarks and the wide decks, together with the feeling of security and strength, had been exciting beyond description. Now when we went below the wide cabin was so obviously the genuine article that even Hervey commented that fishing smacks made the idea of standing-up headroom seem ridiculous. On the Sunday we sailed back and picked up the mooring without trouble and came ashore still delighted, but feeling slightly self-conscious when one or two of the fishermen laughingly asked us how we had made out as smacksmen.

On the following Friday evening I went down early as there was a good deal of clearing up I wanted to do in the hold, and although I turned in fairly late was up early next morning. I had breakfast and cleared up before six and was on deck while the fishermen were still mustering on the hard. I never quite worked out how the mustering was done, but I think the Company men all waited until the Foreman gave the word to go, while the other crews set off as soon as each was complete. Whichever way it was there seemed to be an unwritten rule that no one began setting up sail until the others were ready to do so and this made the getting away of the smacks an impressive spectacle.

Sitting on the *Charlotte*'s rail to watch them I was aware of the pleasure of being on a smack's deck to enjoy this morning parade of fishing smacks and had no thought of myself being out of place. Relaxed and almost, as it were, one of them, I watched the crews make their preparations and hoist sail to get away.

Almost at the same time the activity began down the length of Thornfleet, and the morning stillness became alive to the clatter of windlass pawls and patent sheeves. All down the line of moored smacks sails rose and then for a few moments swung idly until they were sheeted home and filled as each smack got away. Almost in unison the sounds ceased and a score or so of smacks began standing out to sea.

The wind was light south-westerly and the tide was flooding. The smacks made slow going of it coming out and the silence had a hint of intensity. For a moment I wondered if they were racing, but then realized that this was not so. Each of the smacks had got away at the right moment so that they were now sailing in formation. Certainly they were not trying to pass each other, but the same amount of effort was being used in keeping perfect station. Once they were outside in Deeps with more room I had no doubt that, although the Company smacks would hold formation, the others certainly would be racing.

Further in from where the *Charlotte* was lying I heard the hollow note of an exhaust as the *Our Boys* started her engine, and I guessed that Charlie was impatient about how long it would take for the Company smacks to reach their dredging grounds over on the far side of the estuary.

I could see that Charlie was at the tiller, and when his engine had picked up and was running smoothly he sheeted his mainsail in close and began to motor out to the head of the line. After passing the leading smack he swung the *Our Boys* round to come back, and with the tide under him swept down the line until he was behind the hindmost. Here he swung round again and throttled back to begin slowly overtaking. When he reached the first of the Company smacks a towing line was thrown across to him and one of the crew took it and made fast. The smack sheered out of the line to tow astern, and as she did so she ran her staysail down and sheeted in her mainsail flat. Charlie now passed one or two smacks by, but received a line from the next Company smack which sheered out to tow abreast of the first one and lowered her staysail as she did so.

The third Company smack passed her line to the second and sheered out to tow behind her, but as soon as the weight was taken the line was passed over to the first smack. The fourth also passed her line to the second, and sheered out to tow abreast of the third. Similarly the fifth and sixth threw lines across and swept out to tow abreast astern. As soon as Charlie had all his charges towing behind him the sound of the exhaust note quickened as the *Our Boys* began her long tow out to sea.

The steering during this evolution had been flawless and Charlie had gone down the line of smacks taking his pick, without any hailing, and without any of the others being put out to make way for him.

As the *Our Boys* drew towards the *Charlotte* Charlie edged across the creek so that she would pass very close, but paid no attention to me until he was right alongside. He then looked across with a wide grin, and said, 'Sharn't tow any of 'em in again, Mick'. I have no doubt that the wickedness of that thought kept him chuckling for the rest of the morning. In fact, although the towing out was not uncommon, the wind usually freshened as the day wore on, so that towing back was seldom needed.

The remaining smacks made their way out steadily and were soon in the more open water of Deeps, but the morning parade was not quite over as two late-comers were now boarding a little smack further down. In a leisurely way they set up their sails and followed the others out. Later on I found that these two were always about half an hour late and asked Charlie why. He replied by saying they were the Bogus Company and, intrigued, I asked him why bogus. He explained that the firm was in liquidation and was being run by Barclay's Bank. 'Stands to reason it must be bogus, Mick.'

My programme for the morning was to sandpaper and paint the inside of the rails and bulwarks, but the wood was still wet with dew and it was too early to begin. For a time I sat on deck and watched as the smacks reached away down Deeps and then fanned out as each made for its chosen dredging grounds.

The Company boats were making south across the river and I guessed they would begin dredging over on the Bradwell shore, with all of them working a small area. This was one advantage which the Company boats had over the others. Because their grounds were protected they could go straight to the place they wished to work, while all the other smacks which dredged the common ground were obliged to use every artifice to conceal where they caught their oysters. The Company smacks could afford to carry four men dredging and culling all the time, but few of the other smacks carried more than two.

Over the years I have worried often about this artificial handicap but as far as I can see there is no answer to it. If one of the smacks on the common ground should have a good haul from a particular area, she will carry on dredging away from the spot as if nothing unusual had happened, and quite probably will not go near the place again for several days, but even at that one of the others will eventually notice that there is a pattern in her movements, and then two of them will share the secret and it is a valuable one.

In the ordinary course a dredge on the common ground may come up with perhaps twenty or thirty oysters of various sizes in it but, when a find is made, each of the dredges may contain several hundred fully-grown natives. Finds such as this are not all that uncommon and, as long as one smack only knows the place, a good living can be made by visiting it perhaps once a week. When two crews know, it is a matter of days only before the rest catch on, and then the find will be fished out within a day or two. Extra good catches were always concealed but in the end were almost always found out.

As the dew dried off I began my work, and by the time the smacks began to come in I had more than half of my painting done. On Saturday they finished work early and came in soon after eleven more or less together. On the way back from the grounds they did race, and from the time the last dredge was hauled it was a case of devil take the hindmost. Sometimes the smack would go up to the laying so that the day's catch could be relayed direct from her deck, but if the wind were light the catch would be transferred to the boat on the way in, and then one of the crew would take the smack back to the mooring and bring up while the other took the catch off to the laying.

The company smacks had their moorings over the Company layings and for them the relaying of the catch was no problem, but working over their own protected ground they had an interest in trying to keep it clean, and for this reason usually came back with several sacks of limpets, five-fingers and other rubbish which was dumped ashore at the outside end of Packing Marsh. This in itself was quite exciting to watch, as only if the load of rubbish was clearly too much for one load did they ever make two of it, and usually, as the smack came in the sacks would be bundled into the boat with one of the crew who would then cautiously scull her to the dumping ground with no more than perhaps an inch or two of freeboard. I never saw one of the boats sink, but some of them came perilously near to it.

Only a few minutes separated the first smack in from the last one, and within a very short time all were brought up and the crews disappeared for the weekend. I finished my painting and then lounged until it was time to go ashore and collect Hervey. By evening the paint was dry enough for us to get away and sail up to Osea where we lay the night.

I missed the following Saturday for some trivial reason which I cannot remember, but have ever since regretted because on that day Charlie decided on the spur of the moment to go off to the smack with Hervey and show him how to sail her. I heard the tale next day and was sorry indeed to have missed the occasion.

Because I was not present and merely had the tale at second-hand I can now recall only the parts which most roused my envy, but as I gathered it Hervey had met Charlie on the causeway just before high water, and since the wind was hard southerly had made some jocular remark which stirred Charlie into coming off to demonstrate that the *Charlotte* was perfectly handy in the close quarters of the creeks even in near gale conditions.

The pair of them had rowed off to the smack and, brushing aside any suggestion of reefing, Charlie had set full sail. He first turned the smack out to Deeps and then bringing her round let her run back up Thornfleet to the Gut. Here he had brought her round and although he had plenty of water for taking two or three smacks at each tack had scorned such an idea and instead had kept Hervey hard at work on the foredeck while he thrashed the *Charlotte* through each gap in the line. Tack and tack he had wasted no sailing distance and had gauged the whole of the sail down to inches without once giving the impression of cutting things too fine.

Reaching Deeps again he brought the *Charlotte* round and ran back to go up Ditch, but this time with a different idea in mind. By now the tide was nearly level with the salting edge and he told Hervey that in his younger days the boys had vied with each other as to which of them was the better and more daring helmsman. One of their pranks had been to try wending the smacks so close in to the salting edge that rubbing against the 'cant-mud' left muddy marks down the bulwarks. The game was competitive and the longest mud-marks won. On his way back down Ditch he had done this repeatedly and had then peered over the rail to see how long the marks were. Apparently he considered them good enough and was delighted that, in the many years since he had last done it, his hand and eye had lost nothing of their cunning.

At the end of this exhibition he sailed the smack out of Ditch and swept her up to her mooring in one tremendous luff. Hervey had been able to pick up the mooring almost at leisure and haul in enough chain without any hard pulling. The smack had simply sat head to wind waiting for him to do it. Charlie had then helped stow the sails and had afterwards taken Hervey ashore to collect his own dinghy. Back on the hard he had as usual gone off without farewell.

I did not witness any of this myself, and more the pity, but can so easily visualize the perfection of the thing that perhaps I lost nothing of it and in my envy even maybe gained.

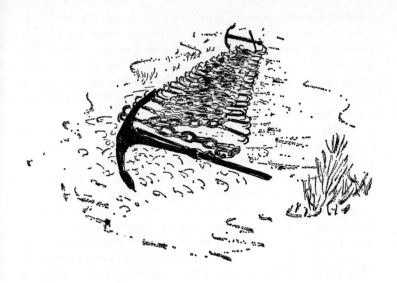

Chapter 8

After his demonstration sail Charlie left us to our own devices and we had to learn from our mistakes. At first we were troubled with getting the *Charlotte* easily in irons and found that when we did this, she would hang in irons and refuse to break away on either tack until we ran the mainsail down. This was undignified, but it happened repeatedly, and after a time we were almost in despair, but then quite suddenly and, for no reason that we ever discovered, she stopped doing it and we had no further trouble with her on that count.

We had been used to the yacht method of having the head-sail sheets led aft to the helmsman, and for a time felt strange with having the jib-sheets on the foredeck, but became used to it and quickly realized how much more purchase one has when working the sail from this position. Even in strong winds we found plenty of time to manage the helm and tend the headsails, and be back aft again as the vessel wended and paid away on the new tack. We began to look on single-handed wending as being a polished and satisfying evolution.

At first we were not used to the barrel windlass, but became adept, and found that it was easy to use and powerful, and was also quick on the occasions that we needed speed. Quite apart from its practical ability, it was satisfying and we soon began to adopt the smacksman's rather flamboyant way of using it.

Within a week or two Hervey produced the *Charlotte*'s new trawl which had been made up for him at Wivenhoe. Neither of us had ever studied a trawl closely and we hauled the new acquisition aloft to look at it and try to fathom out how it worked. It was a long tapering bag of tarred netting, with a trap two thirds of the way down towards the narrow end. The wider, forward end was spread across a wooden beam and a pair of trawl-heads, which were in effect heavy, iron hoops flattened below so that they stood firmly on the deck. The beam was towed on a bridle and warp. This much we could see. Our next task was to find out how to use it.

For the first few weeks our efforts produced nearly as many tangles as fish and we found that putting the trawl over the right way up was not nearly as easy as we expected. Even when it did stay the right way up the net part was often twisted. However we did sometimes get it right and then made good catches of fish which were much envied by the crews of the other boats we sailed with.

At the beginning of the winter the *Bonito* laid up and the two crews then joined forces. Hervey and I would take the smack out on the Saturday, and then in the evening bring her back to Deeps, where we would be joined by Peter and Frank and go straight out again. One of the two crews would turn in and get some sleep ready to take over at dawn. Working on this shift system we were able to keep the smack trawling continuously during most of the weekend, but since a sailing trawler can only tow her net down tide and to leeward we did sometimes have to bring up and wait until a weather-going tide turned again to run in our favour.

The shift system led to great rivalry between the two crews as to which could catch the most fish and the biggest ones. It also led to a good deal of competition as to which crew could give the most accurate position when handing over. Lit buoys were few and far between and on misty nights the navigation was not always easy.

At first we found it difficult to assess how far the smack would tow in a given time and the relieving crew would be given a position which later proved to have been miles in error, but with more experience we began to do better, and before long were not only better at navigating, but began to know from the trawl contents whether or not we were fishing where we thought we were.

In thick weather even the stowboaters were not quite sure of their exact whereabouts and one of them paid us the compliment of asking us if we knew where we were. By good fortune the Bar Buoy was faintly visible in the mist about four hundred yards away. We pointed it out to the skipper who thanked us and sheered away to go into Brightlingsea and probably did not realize how much satisfaction the incident gave us.

Having the two crews on board gave us plenty of scope for wrangling and discussion. Most of our arguments were about boats and on this subject the four of us represented four different views. Hervey believed that barges were the ultimate in sail, while Frank thought that nothing could equal square-rig. Peter maintained that yachts had more virtue than working boats, while I brought up the rear with a solid refusal to hear of anything to the detriment of fishing smacks.

Our wrangles followed a fairly uniform pattern. A discussion would begin in general terms and then narrow down until one of us was defending some barely tenable point of view. This would continue until someone, and usually it was Hervey, would suggest scragging the offender. The differences would then be lost in a free-for-all wrestling match. This was a well-tried system and I do not recall anyone ever being argued out of face.

The others played up to my known views and missed no chance of finding fault with the *Charlotte*, so that my role was usually defensive. Only two of their criticisms caused me much trouble. One was that she was wet in a seaway and

Hervey sometimes complained that she sailed like a half-tide rock. In fact this was unjust and, though she certainly threw up sheets of spray, she kept her decks reasonably dry. I countered that she was never wet when the staysail was down and, if we wished to, she could be made just as dry and probably just as slow as any other boat. He would reply that the barges raced us hands down, which was true enough, but nothing else ever did so. The second complaint was more difficult and concerned her habit of carrying heavy weather helm. Sometimes the *Charlotte* seemed to go out of her way to draw adverse attention to the matter.

On one occasion, Peter's uncle Bruce was with us and had the helm while we were beating back over the tide to repeat a tow. The *Charlotte* wended but instead of bearing away on the new tack came up to wind and lay in irons. We looked round to find out what Bruce was up to and were just in time to see him climbing back on board over the quarter. After wending, he had put the tiller-line over the tiller and had used it to haul the helm to weather, but the line had slipped free so that he went backwards overboard. He had held on to the line and had used it to pull himself back to the rail while the *Charlotte* obligingly lay idle and waited for him. I was delighted that she had behaved herself so capably.

An hour or two later, driving up Deeps on our way in with the *Charlotte* on a tight sheet, we passed close to lee-ward of the Company lighter, and she chose that moment to break her tiller. She luffed, but with commendable quickness Bruce let fly the mainsheet, so that she rose upright, and struck the lighter only a glancing blow. Even at that the blow was heavy enough and her conduct seemed to be perversely indefensible.

This turned the tables on me and I had an uncomfortable amount of ragging for the rest of the evening. Needless to say, I argued back, and this bickering was still going on when we came home. Eventually, Hervey stopped the car as we came to Peat Tye and said that the only thing to do was to debag me and chuck me out. This was done and the car drove off.

There was nothing to be gained by staying on the road to be revealed in the headlights of each car that came by, so without delay I struck off cross-country. In sweater and plimsolls I made good time to Colchester where concealment ended. With no alternative, I decided to make a sprint for it down the lighted streets and hoped that I would not meet anyone I knew.

Several hours later I was woken by a stone thrown against my bedroom window and found the others outside anxious in case I was still at large. They had stopped the car a short distance down the road and, when I did not appear, began a search and had then entered into the spirit of it. They were sure that with the car they could intercept me although I had several alternative roads to use. Eventually they realized that I had eluded them and came to check up and return my bags to me. They chucked them up with a whispered warning that the subject of broken tillers was one to avoid in future.

The following weekend it blew a full gale from the north and, although the river was sheltered and smooth, we found that under two reefs the *Charlotte* towed so hard that the net was difficult to keep on the bottom. She was at ease sailing under two reefs and we did not know that almost always a smack tows better with one more reef than she needs when free. After a rather unsuccessful day we returned in the evening and since there seemed little point in going out again at night we did not bring up in Deeps, but carried on up Thornfleet and picked up the mooring.

We collected Peter and Frank and after lounging and yarning we turned in fairly late. I asked if I could have the dinghy next morning and was told that I could, but must be back on board by nine o'clock.

My dinghy-borrowing was an accepted part of the routine. I was far too interested in things to lie asleep after the sun had risen, and if we brought up for a tide I always took the opportunity to go off on some exploration of my own. At first light next morning I slipped out on deck quietly and, after

71

getting into boots and oilskin, tried to work out where I could go exploring.

The wind was straight down the creek, but from the way the *Charlotte* was sheering about I knew that the flood tide must be running fairly hard. I thought it should be possible to get up to weather and then in the lee of the saltings make a tour of Ditch.

I hauled the dinghy in and made her fast on a short painter while I got into her and set up the rowlocks. I then cast off, but before I had the oars shipped I was already ten or more yards to leeward. I found that by hard rowing I could just make up during the lulls, but when the gusts came I lost nearly all that I had gained. After ten minutes I was still no more than level with the smack though well inshore on the Packing Marsh side trying to keep out of the rougher water. I decided to carry on until I began flagging and then I would run the dinghy ashore on the Packing Marsh and explore the island from end to end. If I began to drop to leeward of the smack I would run the dinghy ashore at once.

In the event, I had several good lulls, and made up about a hundred yards so that I was able to ground the dinghy on the shingle path which led down to the creek from the quay beside the oyster-packing sheds.

Although he never admitted it I was fairly sure that Hervey enjoyed my explorations just as much as I did and on my going back to the smack he always subjected me to an interrogation as to where I had been and what I had done. What had I seen and what construction did I put on it? Needless to say there was always something which he could misconstrue and embroider so that it seemed ridiculous and I had learned by experience that my observations had to be both capable and thorough. Accordingly I walked up the path and began by studying the piles of disused gear stowed away beneath the two sheds. Mostly this was an uninteresting collection of worn-out dredges, but in front of one shed was a large heavily-made iron cage which was covered in barnacles. The use of this I could not work out.

In front of the second shed there were several lengths of

heavy chain, with grapnels secured every two or three feet, and for each chain there was a pair of heavy anchors. I tried to lift one of the anchors, but found that I could only just move it. I guessed that these were the grapnels that the Company laid to protect their beds from thieves.

I next studied the lay of the island. It was a long narrow strip of saltings, straight on the Mersea Fleet side, but slightly convex towards Thornfleet. It ran roughly from north where it was widest towards the south where it ended in a narrow spit covered by high piles of bleaching limpet shell.

At the north end the saltings petered out in a low bank of reeds which gave on to the long spit of the Middle Ooze. This curved away slightly to the west and extended down to the Gut just beyond the causeway. To the south end of the island the saltings were higher and had been protected by wooden shuttering. Being more exposed, the mud spit to the south of the island was shorter and steeper and much firmer than the Middle Ooze.

Closer at hand was a system of oyster-pits which extended from the sheds almost down to the end of the island, but only half a dozen of the nearer ones were still in use. I looked at these. They were shallow oblong pools, just over a foot deep, and were well stocked with some of the largest native oysters I had ever seen. I avoided going too close, as I had no wish to be suspected of oyster-stealing, but even from a range of several yards the pits made a handsome showing. Each of them was planked up with thick elm planks along its ends and sides, and each had a square wooden hove or drain leading to a rill which ran alongside.

I walked along the line of pits and then continued on to make a circuit of the island. At the south end I stopped to look at the heaps of limpet shell and was surprised to notice how many razor and scallop shells there were among the limpets. Most of the scallop shells were of the small size called 'Queens', but a few were nearly of the full 'King Harry' size. I walked back down the Mersea Fleet side and now had the wind and rain in my face. At the Middle Ooze end of the island I paused. It seemed to me that I had not found very much to report on my return to the *Charlotte* and I looked round for something else to make the expedition sound more worthwhile.

Fairly well down the Middle Ooze, on the Thornfleet side, was a small laid-up smack. She was lying over heavily and her stern was raised while her bows were down. She looked uncomfortable, but something about her caught my imagination and I decided to walk down the spit to study her.

As I approached her I began to see that her lines were good. I would not have considered boarding a smack in commission, but this one for all her shapeliness looked very laid-up and forlorn and, without giving the matter a thought, I slipped out of my boots beside her rigging and climbed up to reach her deck. As far as I can recall I had never taken this kind of liberty before, but it did not occur to me that I was trespassing.

She was listing too much for me to move about easily on her deck, but I was able to make my way down her scuppers to her taffrail, and then pulled myself up so that I could sit on her starboard quarter. It was an exposed vantage point, but strong winds can be intoxicating, and perhaps that was partly why everything about her seemed to be so exactly right. She was the right length and the right width, and although totally different from the *Charlotte* was completely in harmony with herself.

The surroundings were right too. Heeling over as she was, with the creek white with surf just below, it was not difficult to imagine she was sailing. Her tiller was lying beside her hold-hatch almost asking to be picked up and slipped into her rudder. The tide was rising quickly, however, and my boots beside her rigging were by now nearly in the water. I clambered along the weather rail and then slid down to the hold-hatch and felt the weight of the tiller, before sliding down to the lee rail on my way back to the rigging and my boots. I retrieved these and pulled them on, and then dropped overboard to the mud. Before leaving her I went round to her stern to read her name and port of registry. She was the *Boadicea* and the port of registry was spelt 'Couchester'. I wondered whether this was a misprint or whether it had been a fair attempt at spelling out the local way of pronouncing the town's name. I noticed that the registry was on a board fastened over some original carving and wondered what the first port had been.

It was time to be getting back to the dinghy, but with the wind now behind me this was not far to go and I reached it quickly. Similarly the drift back to the *Charlotte* took only a few moments and I was still full of the *Boadicea* when I had shed my boots and oilskin and slipped down into the *Charlotte*'s cuddy. I began getting breakfast ready and someone sleepily asked me what I had been doing this time. I gave him a brief account, but possibly some guardedness on my part alerted him, and when I had described my visit to the smack he asked suspiciously what her name was. I told him and with mock incredulity he said he did not believe it. Even I could not be such a fool. Everyone knew she was wider than she was long and so slow that a breath of wind would stop her. Her antecedents were unknown and generally distrusted. In any case she was reputed to be haunted.

The others joined in and foolishly I tried to defend her and quickly became involved. Clutching at straws I recalled the tiller and unwisely said that if the *Charlotte* contrived to break all her spares we might ask if we could borrow it. This was pounced on and the fat was in the fire.

Hervey had not joined in this nonsense but now he swung his feet out and sat up. I was the worst mate he had ever had on board and was a disgrace to the whole fleet, but for all that it was breakfast time. The breakfast was in fact ready and I served it up to them. We settled down to our bacon and eggs and sausages and for the time being the subject of the *Boadicea* was dropped.

They never forgot, however, and from that time on, if I was ever so foolish as to mention a boat's lines I was at once ragged, and reminded about my narrow escape from the fascinations of the *Boadicea*. In this way they gradually built up a kind of fable that one day I would inevitably succumb to her attractions.

Chapter 9

Our discussions were not confined to wrangling about the rival merits of different kinds of boats. The *Charlotte* had opened up for us a wide range of new activities and new experience. We had much to learn and much to talk about.

The trawl itself and the mastering of its ways was a whole new exercise, and we quickly began to learn how to clear the net on deck at night so that it would go over the side cleanly. We learned how to keep the warp clear for running and yet out of the way so that the ordinary activities of the boat could be carried on unimpeded, and we also learned that these ordinary activities could be done much more efficiently so that they did not interfere with the trawl and its gear. This was only the first of our problems however and beyond that we had to learn how to make a sailing vessel work, which is quite a different art from knowing merely how to sail her.

Our method of finding out was trial and error, backed up

by observation of how the crews of the working smacks did it and a good deal of helpful advice from them. They seemed to have a knack of knowing exactly what we were up to even when they were hull-down on the horizon. When we next met them they would almost always be able to tell us what we had done wrongly on such and such an occasion and how we should have set about doing it.

A sailing trawler works with the tide and only exceptionally does she tow her gear behind her. Almost always she works broadside on to the wind and tide and is usually more or less hove-to while working. I say more or less because there are any number of variant combinations of sail areas which can be employed and altered at will to adjust the amount of pull the vessel is exerting.

When the vessel is in this broadside-on working attitude she is referred to as being 'put-to', and the term goes back beyond memory. It is an apt term and means simply that she has been put to work.

A distinction should be drawn between the act of putting-to and the steady state of being put-to which results. The one is a complex evolution, while the other is a state of moving equilibrium relatively easy to maintain.

The evolution took us years to learn and, even when learned, practice allows it to be polished until it becomes one of the most graceful manoeuvres in the whole of seamanship. In contrast the steady state can be maintained by simple rule of thumb.

It would be out of place to describe the act of putting-to in detail when talking about our trawling of that first winter, but in broad outline, the trawl is made ready in the lee scuppers. At the time of putting-to the vessel is wended to come round hove-to on the other tack and while she does so the net is cleared over the side. After she is round the vessel will be making more leeway than forward way, so the net streams clear on the weather quarter. When it has streamed to its full length it opens out rather like a parachute and at that moment the beam is pushed over the side and the warp is lowered away until the trawl reaches the bottom.

Our early attempts at doing this were very ragged, and in effect what we did was to get the smack put-to somehow, and then no matter how crudely we had done it we were able to enjoy the new pleasures of what I have come to look on as the fourth state of a sailing vessel. This is not by any means fanciful and the state of being put-to is quite unlike anything else in sailing.

If the first state of a sailing vessel is when she is brought up, the second would be when she is under way and sailing. The third would be when she is hove-to with her energies curbed and the fourth when she is put-to and harnessed to her gear. Each of the four states is a clear-cut situation with a clear-cut set of seamanship rules. The fourth state was to us a new experience with new pleasures to find out and new rules to learn. We began finding out both and quickly realized that the state of being put-to has much to commend it.

When put-to the *Charlotte* seemed to undergo a change of character. When sailing in the ordinary way she was lively and even boisterous. In hard winds she was able to claw her way quickly up to windward over a foul tide and, particularly when she was doing this at night, it needed little imagination to picture the old days of the salvage smacks. If in the same conditions she were now put-to she became at once docile and very nearly silent. Even in strong winds the noise of a sailing vessel approaching her could be heard quite a long way off.

The quietness and easy motion when she was put-to gave an immediate sense of comfort, and with that went a sense of security which was for the most part due to contrast.

When towing her gear the smack moved down tide to lee-ward at the same speed with the tide. She was thus moving relatively slowly in a known direction and if she deviated from this she at once gave warning of the change. If she began to tow too hard she fore-reached and luffed, but if she began towing too slowly the tide swept her head round so that she payed away. If she towed out of the channel her warps at once revealed the changing depth of water and if an unlit buoy appeared in her path evasive action could be taken without need for undue hurry. Passing an unlit buoy while towing barely called for comment, but the same buoy passed on the way back while sailing fast to windward, would be reported at once by name, together with its bearing and its distance.

We were immediately aware that being put-to gave us more leisure to enjoy the boat than we usually had while sailing her and we delighted in the fact that we now had no need to be for ever on the way to somewhere. The *Charlotte* was happy enough where she was and was doing her rightful work in the way she was designed to do it, with no fuss and no great exertion on our part. No longer did we trace out thin lines across the water and seek to justify them by the pleasures we hoped to find at a destination. Instead we found a new pleasure in the breadth and the depths of the water round us.

Our new-found leisure to enjoy the smack took many forms. Sometimes we would just sit on deck and yarn, or perhaps would be getting on with various jobs about the boat while we kept casual watch on what she was doing. Perhaps most of all we enjoyed the last hour before daylight when the outlines of the smack changed from black to grey and then, as the sun lifted, quickly lit with colour. In the surroundings of a hazy winter dawn the *Charlotte* was colourful, and richly so. Red decks, red sails and the gleam of spars, while outboard the facets of the sea reflected the sunlight, red as copper.

Usually the rising of the sun was the time to change watches and the signs and sounds of life from the watch below served to dispel some of the dawn's remoteness. The smoke from the cabin stove would increase and roll outboard across the rail to blow away so low on the water that it seemed almost to follow the lifting of the swell. From the hatchway would come the sounds and smell of bacon frying and, all in all, the smack would seem the embodiment of our wishful ideas of a vessel at home on the sea and at ease with it with only the minimum of tending.

In those days it was the usual custom for fishing boats to keep a light handy so that it could be shown if any other vessel came too close, but no lights were set in the ordinary course. This was partly to preserve night vision and the professional fishermen did have extraordinarily good night vision, but at least as much it was done to avoid attracting other fishing boats to an area where fish had been found.

Being on board at night and travelling at the same speed as the tide we were able to enjoy being close neighbours with the sea. Sometimes the sea is silent and seems almost deserted, but usually it is teeming with life, and particularly at night small unexplained noises are going on all round. A sailing vessel put-to and silent in the water, without lights and without the disturbing vibration of an engine, does not alarm nearby creatures, and quite often a flock of geese or other birds would be heard coming nearer until at last one bird would appear alongside a few feet away, and then seeing the smack would alarm the others and the whole flock would take wing to move perhaps fifty yards and then put down again.

Gradually we came to identify the various sounds which went on round us, and usually as daylight approached we would keep extra quiet in the hope of seeing our neighbours before they noticed us and made away. Each new sound identified meant a new pleasure on succeeding nights.

Not all of our neighbours were pleasant however, and sometimes at dawn we would be subjected to the sight of gulls taking toll of small migrating birds and, having watched this slaughter, I have sometimes wondered how small migrating species have ever survived at all. We watched one herring gull take three golden crested wrens in as many seconds and there were thousands of gulls feeding at the same speed. I can hardly imagine that many of the wrens reached the security of land that morning.

Over the years I have watched gulls feeding in this way several times, but strangely enough only in the Raysand, which makes me think that this stretch of water lies on one of the main flight-lines of migrating birds.

The Raysand was one of our regular areas of work because the set of the tide always has some north and south in it, whereas in the main tideways the set is roughly east and west. Since a sailing trawler cannot tow her gear to windward we were often glad to work the lee-going tide in the main channels and then sail over to the Raysand to make a cheating haul there during the unfavourable tide.

This was fair enough in reasonable weather, but if the wind were hard westerly the Buxey was an uncomfortable neighbour to have close to leeward on a dark night, and in these conditions we usually reached into Brightlingsea to spend the flood tide brought-up in the creek. This had the added attraction that it allowed us to watch the stowboats come in soon after dawn. If they had made good fishing they would often be loaded down until their decks were awash amidships, and in rough weather this made an impressive sight which lent force to some of the tales we had heard of the old sailing stowboaters filling at the Shipwash or perhaps the Tongue and then racing home to win the market.

I had heard from several of the men that one smack had raced home under full sail and with a jack-yard topsail set, but had gone to the bottom in Brightlingsea Creek when the boy gave her the anchor chain too quickly and she snubbed. The smacks now worked under engine, but the men had all worked in the days of sail and were well worth talking to. Watching the smacks come in and then talking to the men while they waited for the skiffs to come alongside was more realistic than hearing the same tales in a pub.

By way of finding opportunity to yarn with the stowboat crews we often took the dinghy alongside to beg a bucketful of sprats and found the men amiable and easy to get along with. Their hardiness was proverbial, but it needed to be seen to be fully appreciated. On one occasion when I was miserably wet and cold although clad in oilskin and sou'wester, the men were working on deck in guernseys and peaked caps without showing any sign of discomfort.

I asked the skipper if he ever wrapped up at all against the wet. He straightened his back with a grin, and said that once you were used to it you barely noticed it. He was quite affable about the question and did not resent it He told me that as a youngster his first job on board had included the tending of the jib-sheets, and in rough weather that really was wet work. He would have felt a fist or a boot if he had flinched, but did not recall that he had ever needed such encouragement.

We were not as hard as that and did try to keep dry if at all possible, though we noticed sometimes that once we gave up trying the wet was not nearly so worrying. On the whole, wet worried us far more than cold and that was one of the early discoveries of that first winter. We found that the *Charlotte*'s exposed open decks were not nearly as cold as we expected and concluded that, being free to move about at will, we were better able to keep warm than we should have been cooped up in the close quarters of a yacht's cockpit.

Cold hands worried us during rowing and using the leadline for any length of time, but strangely, hauling in the trawl was much less cold to the fingers. We all suffered from chapped hands and wrists and quite often the backs of my own hands would still be swollen by the time the next weekend came round. It was not until some years later that I discovered that a light dressing of tallow on the halyards prevented this chapping and made my hands much easier to keep clean.

This was the first winter that any of us had seriously attempted winter sailing and added to that is the fact that quite a lot of our sailing was done at night in weather which was sometimes far from fine. However, my chief recollection of the period is one of pleasure at the comfort and easy life on board the *Charlotte*. Admittedly we always had a fire going and spent a good proportion of our time in front of it, but even at that we soon hardened off so that the weather did not worry us unduly. Possibly we were a bit vainglorious about this, but during the last snowstorm of the season we met our match and were cut neatly back to size. This did us all good and I still enjoy the recollection.

We had been trawling in Eagle Deep in quest of cod, which the older fishermen told us had always been there in years gone by. By about midday it was clear that we were not doing well and when the net came up empty yet again we decided that as it had begun to snow heavily we would make our way home. Visibility was poor and we sighted nothing until we were well inside Deeps and were quite proud of the achievement. We brought up and lazed about for a time, and then later went ashore with the idea of spending an hour in the Victory. When we got there the bar was not yet open and it was too cold to hang about. For want of anything better, we decided to pass the time by going down to the saltings to look round the boats laid-up in the mud-berths.

The snow was laying thick and, being exposed, the saltings were far from warm. We trudged down the lines of boats passing more or less disparaging comments about this stern or that bow, until close to the creek-edge we found a small schooner which was undeniably attractive. She had a truly beautiful clipper-bow and her rigging was still standing. Her masts raked well aft and looked convincingly traditional. Intrigued, we stopped to look at her and decided to venture up her gang-plank to study her more closely.

There was no sign of anyone on board and, greatly daring, we went on deck. While we were looking at her shrouds and dead-eyes, the hatch opened and an elderly man put out his head and shoulders. He asked us what we were doing and did not sound very pleased to see us.

We apologized for our intrusion, and added truthfully that we had been so attracted by his schooner that we had been unable to resist coming on board to look at her.

This reply seemed to mollify him and in a more friendly tone he asked us if we would care to come below to see her accommodation. We accepted delightedly and, quickly shedding boots and oilskins, followed him down the companion to the saloon below.

He made us welcome and roared the fire up for a moment or two and then opened it. We all sat round it toasting our hands and feet. He talked to us about schooners and he spoke easily and well. He began by citing Stevenson's belief that the only worthwhile use of money was the owning of a schooner and endorsed this sentiment.

He thought that the schooner rig was the most seaworthy man had been able to devise. It had not been equalled, and would never be surpassed. Nowadays people sometimes said that the rig was out of date, but this was nonsense. This or that generation might not have need for it, but the rig would never be out-moded. It was timeless.

He paused for a few moments and then in a less certain voice began to deplore the fact that the rig was going through a period of less than proper recognition. The reason for this was not far to seek. Modern youth had grown so soft and so lacking in the traditions of the sea, that none of them were able to stand up to any extremes of weather. The rig began where they gave up.

Somewhat unwisely, but moved I am sure only by sympathy with the old man's sorrow, Hervey ventured to point out that on the *Charlotte* we sailed every weekend regardless of the weather. This statement did not abate the old man's misery. He tried to recall when there had last been any weather, and told us that as far as his memory would serve him, there had not been any weather worthy of the name since we'd been in our cradles.

He gave us no chance to recuperate from this, but carried on without pause, but now using a different tone again. He did not bother with citing farflung ports and described no wild horizons, nor did he talk of the names of boats and how they behaved in famous gales. The whole argument was impersonal. Simply he gave us a judicial survey of the reason why one vessel could live while the one next to her foundered.

I cannot recall now anything of the arguments he used, but the effect of his words is with me yet. For the first time I began to realize that beyond the enjoyment of mere weather there is an unwritten science of seamanship which goes beyond the ordinary calls and comes into its own when a lesser knowledge would abandon hope. Right or wrong I came away with the belief that everything which a boat does needs to be understood and thought about so that the helmsman and the boat almost fuse to become a single entity.

After a time he stopped talking and there was a short period of casual conversation. We rose to take our leave and thanked him for so kindly entertaining us. On deck we resumed our boots and oilskins and said goodbye to him.

We trudged our way across the saltings to the road. The Victory was open now but did not attract us and no one suggested going in. We passed it by, each of us still occupied with the old man's words.

Chapter 10

During the winter we heard rumours that Stan, who was one of the founder members of the fleet, had decided to buy the *Snowdrop* which was a rather larger fishing smack than the *Charlotte*. This was disquieting.

We had already had several strenuous arguments with him about the merits and what he claimed to be the faults of the smack hull, rig and trim. Although we did not suppose that he believed half the things he said, it was obvious that if he had a smack to apply them to, he would certainly set out to produce something better than the traditional smack.

Furthermore, he would claim that the *Charlotte* was now outclassed and would spare no pains to prove it. The *Charlotte* would be on the defensive, with all the troubles which that involved. We heartily wished that he had bought something slower and less formidable than the *Snowdrop*.

Just before Easter the *Bonito* crew split away to fit out the *Bonito* and resume independent sailing and, on the *Charlotte*, Hervey and I spent two weekends fitting out. We replaced all the running rigging and increased the weight of it, partly because the smack had before been rather lightly rigged, but undoubtedly the threat of the *Snowdrop* had some part in it. Either way, when the fitting out was done the *Charlotte* was in good fettle to stand up to hard sailing.

Shortly after the refit the *Snowdrop* came out and Stan laid a mooring in Mersea Fleet. He had put an engine in and had made a handsome cabin. He had also fitted her with a brand new trawl. We were invited to look at her and on the Saturday afternoon rowed round the spit of the Packing Marsh to make our visit.

Stan showed us the new trawl and, to allow us to see it better, hauled the end aloft so the net blew out lightly on the wind. The slender cotton mesh was newly cutched to a lovely russet colour, and the shape was perfect. We praised it with all the truthfulness of envy. This was not enough however and we were challenged to a trawling match next day. We had no alternative but to accept, which we did, and then after a few minutes of banter took our leave and rowed back round the island to the *Charlotte*.

We were not happy about the challenge and wished we could avoid it. We knew quite well that the rivalry was superficial, but it was a waste of time to be involved in competition trawling when there were so many other interesting things waiting to be done.

During the ensuing weeks the *Charlotte* and the *Snowdrop* fought an undeclared battle for supremacy, but friendships were not affected, and during the whole period we yarned and argued in each other's cabins as a matter of course. Later, when the battle was long forgotten, it was Stan that I turned to in the first instance when I wrecked the *Boadicea*, and he came to help with no question or delay. Allowing all that, the struggle while it lasted was fought out in good earnest.

In the evening we went over to the Victory and our reception there did not improve our spirits. We had lent the *Charlotte*'s trawl to the *Waterwitch* some weeks before, when she had lost hers on some sunken wreckage. The trawl had been returned to the *Charlotte*'s deck, but we had not seen the crew since to hear how they had got along with it. From having seen the *Snowdrop*'s new trawl we knew that ours which was second-hand and often tarred, was not the best net in the world, but we were not prepared for the joyous rudery with which the *Waterwitch* crew hailed our entrance.

They bought us a pint each and proposed Hervey's health, as the lineal descendant of Stringbag the Sailor. They also composed an impromptu ditty in honour of him and chanted it with energy. Hervey took this in his stride and maintained good-humouredly that our net caught just as many fish as anybody else's, but this caused so much merriment that we gave up and joined in the laughter with them.

Later, as we rowed back to the *Charlotte* we agreed that things did not look rosy for the challenge match next day, but there was nothing we could do about it.

At tide-time next morning the two smacks slipped away down Deeps and the match was on. Our best chance was to keep clear of the *Snowdrop* in the hope of being lucky finding fish, and at the end of the tide we had done more than moderately well, but as we turned up the river tack for tack behind her we knew that we had not done well enough. The only matter in issue was the size of our defeat.

After bringing up, we hove the net aloft to dry and decided that we might as well get the thing over and be done with it. We sculled the dinghy ashore and walked over the crest of the Packing Marsh to hail the *Snowdrop* lying in the fleet beyond. We asked how the new net had worked out and in reply were told that it had caught thirty-five soles, sixteen plaice and a hundred and thirty-seven dabs. This was unanswerable, but something about the counted dabs stung and we dulled the edge in a short exchange of insults. We walked back across the island. There was nothing to be said and we were both quiet.

After we had cleared up and stowed the gear we rowed

ashore and shared out our catch at the top of the cause-way. Hervey said that we might as well stop at the Peldon Rose for a pint of 'elevenses', our local bitter. This was a usual cure for fisherman's luck and I hoped it would be effective this time.

No more was said about the trawling until just before we parted, and then he made a heartfelt comment about the *Snowdrop* and all her sanguinary works. I took this as a sign of recovery and easily agreed.

The following weekend he arrived with a brown-paper parcel tightly tied with rather luxurious looking string and we opened it on deck to reveal a new trawl-net of nut-brown cotton. It was almost silky in its softness and when we hauled it aloft to bend it the wind caught it lightly. When it was bent it set beautifully and we could find no fault with it.

After that we did more or less keep level-pegging with the *Snowdrop* as far as trawling was concerned, but the question of speed was a different matter since the *Snowdrop* was reputed to be the second fastest smack in Mersea. Other things being equal she could race the *Charlotte* easily, but we did our best to prevent that kind of equality arising. This meant that we tended to reef later than we would have done without the rivalry and we began to gain experience in hard sailing which we might not otherwise have found.

At the time we were dubious about the good seamanship of this, but were less at fault than we supposed. Usually, when a smack is acquired as a yacht, her new owner is dissatisfied with her lack of freeboard and her unaccustomed stiffness and, reacting to this, he takes out half her ballast so that she now becomes high-sided and has the appearance and easy motion of a yacht. In the *Charlotte* we had left the ballast as it was. She sat very low in the water and was vigorously stiff. Our hard driving embarrassed her very little and we began to find out that she had far more reserve than even we had given her credit for.

Late in the spring the smack-yacht owners organized a race and courtesy required that the *Charlotte* should enter.

Neither of us was enthusiastic. The *Charlotte* was unconverted and not improved upon and this was a gospel and a creed. We valued allegiance with the proper smacks and were chary of losing the one connection by over-free liaison with the other. That much was obvious but beyond it was something more difficult to define. A feeling that sailing for competition's sake was an alien devotion.

Whatever the reasons, the smack-yacht race did not appeal. We agreed that in fairness to the *Charlotte* she must be properly scrubbed, but we did not accept that we must carry a racing crew. We would sail her as we always sailed her and, given wind, that was all she needed.

On the Saturday we put the *Charlotte* on the hard and scrubbed her, and then on the night tide laid her off in Deeps. When we woke in the morning there was enough wind to please anybody and as we had breakfast we commented wrily that having hoped for wind we could hardly grumble now we had it.

Later, we turned out to tidy up after being on the hard and in view of the weather thought it would be sensible to clear the deck of as much loose gear as possible. It was getting late, but we decided that there was still time for me to take the legs ashore and dump them. While I was doing this, Hervey would put one reef in the mainsail and bend the number two jib. We had thought about putting two reefs in the main, but reluctantly had given up that idea.

The row in against the wind was slow and by the time I reached the inshore end of Cob I was beginning to worry about getting back in time. I decided to take a short cut across Bussand to land the legs on the quay beside the *Victory*. To my surprise I found Charlie waiting to help me lift the legs ashore and very anxious about me being late back for the start. This put a different complexion on the race and I realized that our loyalty to the proper smacks was not in doubt.

I asked him what rig he recommended for the day and for a moment he was troubled. He looked at the sky thoughtfully and, for a second or two remained undecided, but then his face cleared and he swung the dinghy round to head out and gave her a good shove-off. As he did so he gave me a wide grin and said, 'Give her one, Mick.' He then turned and walked away towards the road.

The phrase 'give her one' was local jargon for setting whole sail in rather too much wind and, rowing back towards the *Charlotte*, I expected trouble about this new advice. There was no time to waste and before I was fully alongside I told Hervey what Charlie had advised. For a moment he did not believe it and briefly argued that Charlie had meant one reef, but he knew better and was already beginning to untie the reef-points. He told me to rouse out the big jib and be quick about it. We made the change and were away just in time for the first gun.

When the anchor was at the davit I catted it securely and, following up that thought, I put a sail tyer lashing round the kedge on the starboard rail. Hervey had meanwhile let the dinghy go on her anchor and we joined in the jockeying.

There were three other smacks starting and all were reefed. All were jockeying under jib and main and were sailing fast. We took a good deal of ragging about our whole mainsail, but were too busy to pay much attention.

The first leg was to Seaview Buoy and we made a good start with the wind on the port quarter. As we crossed the line I set the staysail and felt the surge as it filled. Despite its small area a smack's working staysail is a very pressing sail.

Having a whole mainsail and the wind aft of the beam, the *Charlotte* had a clear advantage and by the time we were half way to the buoy we were so far ahead that we remarked that if we could only get round the course without disaster the race was already in our pocket.

We were well aware that avoiding disaster was more easily said than done and began planning the gybe we would need to make when we reached the buoy. We thought it was essential that the gybe should be made on a very tight sheet and arranged to combine forces to haul the sheet in until it was straight up and down, when I would belay it. Hervey would then gybe the smack and after the impact was absorbed I was to ease the sheet out checking it as much as possible.

The gybe when it came was heavy, but all the gear held. I had been anxious that if I let the belaying take the whole impact the sheet might jam and, during the moment when the sail was slack overhead, I shortened in the bight of the belaying to a bare minimum. The gybe itself cleared the rest of it, but expended the greater part of its force in doing so. Only the tail part of the impact came full on my hands. It was heavy and I lost a fraction, but then was able to hold it.

As the *Charlotte* felt the gybe she strove to luff and I knew that just forward of me Hervey was using full helm to check her. The perilous part of any gybe is the luff which follows when the vessel has been stung with the impact and I knew that much depended on not easing any sheet away until the smack was controlled and answering her helm.

The moment of a gybe is silent, and as the *Charlotte* fought for her head outside sounds were stilled. For a moment she almost won and luffed a fraction. The weight on the sheet increased and now I could barely hold it. With some detached faculty I listened to, and judged, the swirl of water in the rudder-trunk. Not until the swirling eased must she be allowed any sheet at all.

It was a full two seconds before Hervey mastered her and then suddenly the rudder-trunk was silent. I began checking out sheet, hand over fist, and as the sail came fuller to the wind the weight increased. Hervey turned to take some of the weight with me and we continued checking out. When about half the sheet was gone, he began to let the smack luff and then, leaving the helm for me to manage with my knee, was away forward to tend the headsails.

The helm was light enough by now and keeping the smack away was not a problem, but the weight on the sheet was more than I could check alone and the last fathom tore itself out willy nilly. The boom fetched up heavily at the end of it, but by good fortune nothing parted and no harm was done. Hervey came aft again and took the helm.

The second leg was across the river to the buoy off St

Peter's Point, and for the moment we could not see it. In the deeper water to leeward the sea was running too high and with too much spindrift. I went forward and stood on the pin-rail in the weather rigging and from this position saw it. We were near enough on course.

I came down and went aft to rejoin Hervey. For the moment we now had time to spare and glanced aft to see how the others had got on. We found we were alone. Hull down beneath the spume we could see the other three smacks in a cluster without a mainsail left between them.

For a fraction of a second I think we both felt irritation and Hervey was already luffing, but then bore away again and said they all had engines and were on the weather shore. They could help themselves. He went on to say that in theory we could reef now and sail round the course at leisure. This was unthinkable and we agreed to carry on, but possibly we both overlooked that running to leeward as we were, we had not yet felt the full weight of the wind.

We were by now well out across the deeper water and there could be no denying that the sea was shorter and steeper than was comfortable, but we rounded the second buoy without trouble and found that we could make a close fetch of the third leg back to Deeps.

Going to windward the *Charlotte* usually lifts her head to each sea just before she reaches the crest of it and, when sailing in this way, breaks through each one in turn surrounding herself in spray. While doing this she looks as if she should be wet, but in fact keeps her decks fairly dry.

On this occasion she found a different stride and, setting her head down at the outset, she kept it down. Partly perhaps, this was due to the form of the sea, which was short and steep with a good deal of broken water on the crests, but much more it was due to her being pressed so that she had almost no reserve of buoyancy in her head. Whatever the reason, she did not lift but instead sailed through the seas.

From the rigging forward she submerged herself in water, but was heeling enough to spill it as quickly as it came inboard across her bows and, spilling it in this way, it did not oppress her. She did not feel soggy or borne down with the weight of it. She did not heel unduly, but put her lee rail down until it was awash amidships and at this angle felt stiff.

Hervey had put a double turn on the tiller line but watching, I thought that the *Charlotte* was carrying a good deal less weather helm than usual and I put this down to the fact that her quarters were raised relative to her head, which would improve her metacentric balance.

The water coming over her bows was washing loosely-stowed things down her deck and I went forward to begin securing them, but Hervey shouted to me to come aft again and not to be a fool.

The two anchors were secured and did not shift, but apart from those two, everything else stowed forward of the hatches went. First one thing and then another washed down to the lee rail where it floated outboard and then suddenly was caught up and swept away astern.

By good fortune we were on the starboard tack so the anchor chain was not at risk. At that time neither of us knew that in rough weather the smacksmen feared the anchor chain and always lashed it. If it crossed the deck and burst outboard through the bulwarks the smack could well founder if being hard driven.

When we had cleared the main tideway and were in rather smoother water we had a short rainsquall which made the smack heel a trifle more but did not otherwise affect her very much, but it did show us the amount of wind that a fishing smack can take when she is moving fast. At the height of the squall Hervey leaned across and bellowed in my ear that this was the sail of a lifetime.

We were in the shallows again now, and then almost too soon were in the shelter of Deeps with the finishing line ahead. We saw the smoke of the gun and waved to acknowledge it.

Hervey wended and I ran the staysail down. The *Charlotte* came up hove-to and almost motionless. We put two reefs in the main and then hove her to again under the staysail while we changed jibs. Docile under reduced canvas she paid away and wended and we carried on up Deeps. We retrieved the dinghy and then beat back to the mooring which we picked up uneventfully.

Later we rowed ashore and Charlie came down the causeway to meet us. As we rounded up the dinghy beside him he grasped the gunwale and said, 'Never for a moment thought you'd go and do it', but the pleasure in his face was a reward. As far as I know he never spoke of the race outside that one comment.

Chapter 11

Hervey's affection for sailing barges led him to spend a good deal of his leisure time at Francis and Gilders's barge-yard which was just up-river of Colchester Hythe Bridge. One evening he suggested that I should go down with him. I accepted the invitation and, not having any idea of what the yard would be like, went down full of curiosity.

I did not realize that one of the necessities of a barge-yard is an area of clean grass on which sails can be spread out for repair and re-dressing and was surprised to find that the yard was in one corner of a clean, open meadow hidden away in the centre of Colchester dock area.

Like many other Colchester people I had no idea that this oasis existed in the middle of such drably industrial surroundings, but just as surprising as the field itself was the activity going on there. As we walked over the grass, picking our way between sails I saw a small group of men in front of one of the sheds. We joined them and I gathered that the shipwrights were bending a huge baulk of oak which was propped up with a weight hanging from its outboard end.

About one third down its length the oak was swathed in wet sacks. Under the sacks a small, bright fire was burning. We were told that the fire had been going for three days and nights but there was great excitement at the moment as the wood was beginning to bend and before long the fire would be shifted inboard to adjust the curve. A template was leaning against the shed but I gathered that this was merely to check the final bend. The real work was all done by eye.

On this occasion one of the circle was not there but was away ill at home, and somehow the suggestion arose that Hervey should sail the *Charlotte* round to Paglesham to pay a call on him.

Coming home later in the evening we discussed this idea further and it was agreed that we would make the trip during the coming weekend. We decided that we would make the passage without using any spoken words of command. Ordinary conversation could go on as usual, but the sailing must be done simply by meshing in together.

This idea was the product of one of our many discussions. Hervey maintained, and I agreed with him, that real skill at any trade is almost always associated with sparingness of words. We had for some time been using only the minimum of words, but it was a new departure to attempt a whole passage without having recourse to them at all. It promised to be an interesting experiment and would be good training for me.

We started early on the Saturday morning with a moderate to fresh southerly breeze and fetched away down to the Swire Hole and then took the flood through the Raysand. Doing without spoken commands was stimulating and I found that in effect I was constantly acting as a kind of shadow-skipper, who must always be about two seconds ahead. For example it was difficult to wend the *Charlotte* as smoothly as she should be wended if the first warning that I had was Hervey putting the helm down, but equally it was undignified to go forward more than a second or two early.

After a time it began to work out very well and it cut both ways. If he let the jib shake I could either ignore it or I could harden in the sheet, but if he let it shake twice the sheet came in anyway and with a broad grin to discomfort him.

Similarly, if I thought he had too little water I could pick up the lead and take a sounding and he could either carry on or wend at his discretion, but if he lashed the helm and took a sounding himself, I could take it I was slacking.

By the time we were beating up the Roach we had discovered various ways of communicating without the use of words. Leaning in the lee rigging I could see more clearly than he how near or far we were from the edge of the deeper water and, if I looked aloft and then at the water and casually began to move forward to tend the jib, he would wend at once, but if I continued lounging in the rigging he would carry on for a second or two longer.

We began to realize that, without any insubordination, we were sailing with two skippers each lending his full attention to making the execution as near flawless as was possible. Probably we never did sail the *Charlotte* better than on that day. We both enjoyed the sail and when we went ashore to make his call he picked up the same theme again as we walked up Paglesham Lane.

He told me a tale about the shipyard we had looked at as we came ashore. It belonged to two brothers who worked on the same principle of sparingness of words. When they had a barge building, the elder brother built the starboard side and the younger one the port, and they prided themselves that from the time the keel was laid, until the time the barge was launched, they did not need to discuss their work at all.

This tale caught my imagination and as we walked back down the lane after his visit I was still thinking of it. It seemed to me that the two brothers had hit on an ideal way of acting watchdog to each other without friction, I also thought they had discovered a way of communicating far more fulfilling than mere discussion.

In the lane the sun was almost too hot, but as we came back to the saltings the breeze was fresh and cool and for a few minutes we sat on the seawall looking at the *Charlotte*.

I knew that Hervey had some reading to do and wanted to get on with it. I suggested that he should go back on board, while I would stay on shore to leave him in peace. I would do some exploring and then come back to the wall and keep an eye open for him when he came on deck. He agreed with this and we parted company.

At first I examined the oyster-pits which were more solidly built than any I had seen before and seemed to have chalk floors. I noticed that the wooden hoves draining them were round and were drilled out from a single solid log as opposed to the square built-up hoves of the Mersea oyster-pits.

I then went along the wall to the point at which it turns inland along the side of Paglesham Creek. I decided not to go any further but returned a short distance so as to be well in sight of the *Charlotte* and then sat down at the foot of the wall to lounge in the sun.

Out in the river the ebb tide was half way gone and the flat mud was uncovering as a wide strip on either side of the water. The mud was smooth but at intervals small rills ran down from the saltings, and along the rills and the edges of the water, parties of ox-birds were working silently.

Slightly up the river from where I sat, five Company smacks were brought-up in line astern, and at an interval ahead of them the *Charlotte* lay modestly apart, clearly one of them and, as it were, claiming kinship. On the marsh opposite the gulls roosted and overhead the noise of the larks fitted well with the quiet of the saltings.

It was a lazy summer afternoon and lounging on the sea-wall I soon began to doze. Perhaps I even slept, but was woken by the warning note of a redshank near at hand and, still sleepy, heard the ruffle as the gulls on Potten Island roused. I sat up to see what was going on. The crews of the smacks had turned out and were casting off the sail tyers and I supposed that they would be taking the last of the ebb home for the weekend.

Watching the preparations idly, I was curious about the fact that the men had all been on deck when I first sat up and felt sure that the gulls would have put up as soon as the first of them turned out. It seemed to me that on all five boats the men must have come on deck at the same time. I wondered whether there had been some kind of signal between them or whether it was simply a matter of timing. I could imagine a foreman looking at his watch and then saying that it was time to move, but could not believe that any foreman would admit that he had looked at his watch five minutes too soon. There was a mystery about the way professional seamen timed their actions so precisely.

The crew of the leading smack began setting up their sails and I listened to the flat note of the windlass pawls as the anchor chain was shortened in. The sound of the pawls slowed and I knew that the anchor was now on the point of breaking out. The note quickened again as the anchor came free and the smack payed away gracefully on the port tack. The man on the peak halyard had finished hauling at the exact moment that she did this and was now clearing the fall. A moment later he had finished and the smack was shipshape. I guessed that from start to finish the whole evolution had taken just over two minutes.

I expected the smack to bear away at once to begin her run down-river, but she did not do so. Instead she continued on the port tack sailing free and then while still fairly well out from the shore she wended and, still sailing freer than I thought really necessary, continued on up the river. Meantime the crew of the second smack had begun setting up their sails.

The first smack wended again just ahead of the *Charlotte* and the sound of her staysail blowing to leeward came to me at the same time as the quickening of the windlass pawls of the second smack as she payed away on the port tack. The two smacks were now on the same tack and perfectly in station. Meantime the crew of the third smack were beginning to set up their sails.

All thought of sleepiness was gone now and my mind was working quickly. The Company men always worked in formation and prided themselves on their station-keeping, but none of them would ever admit that there was any method in it. If questioned, they would reply evasively, and perhaps say that there was nothing to it, or possibly, would grin and point out that the foreman was a tartar. The nearest I had ever come to having a direct answer was when Charlie himself had told me that it was easy enough if you started right, but later, watching his boats dredging in Thornfleet I had never been able to detect any kind of system in the way they did begin.

Failing in that direction, I had several times spent quite long periods watching his fleet working in formation hoping that one of them would lose station so that I could see how she set about regaining it. Not once had this happened and I concluded that with so many variables to contend with, they could not be relying only on accurate sailing but must be using some rule-of-thumb method of checking their position all the time, but what the method was I could not work out.

That was the background to the present situation and, perhaps because the setting was so perfect, I knew already that this time I was to have the whole method demonstrated to me with no detail neglected. As the two smacks crossed the creek towards me I had already jumped to one conclusion and felt certain that the wending in front of the *Charlotte* was the key to the whole problem. If each smack in turn could wend there at the right moment she would be in station and all the others watching her could adjust so as to be in station with her.

I felt sure that this was the crux of it. Before, I had always supposed that the Company foreman's smack was the master unit and had tried to relate the movements of all the other smacks to her. This had not worked out at all. I could now see that if each smack in turn was master during the few moments while she wended at the datum point this would work out much better. In effect the whole fleet would be given a new datum every second tack and could adjust accordingly.

By the time the two smacks had reached my side of the river I had a tentative system worked out and was ready to make predictions, checking the theory as the scene unfolded.

The two smacks wended and then while the second one

crossed the river in the way I expected, the first one hauled her wind and sailed on up keeping much closer to the near shore.

As I expected the second smack wended just in front of the *Charlotte* and at the same time the first one came round too, running her peak down as she put-to to begin her tow down the length of the laying. I saw her dredges go over and shifted my attention to the third smack. As I expected she was now sailing on the port tack in station with the second one, but in addition I saw that the fourth and the fifth smacks had also got away. These last two were roughly in station, but were clustered together too close to be tidy.

For a moment this puzzled me, but then I realized that being fourth and fifth in line, these two would have further to sail than the three leaders and I guessed that they would be making six tacks before putting-to where the others would be making only four.

The sequence continued to emerge smoothly. The leading smack was towing down hove-to close to the near shore and, as the third smack wended in front of the *Charlotte*, the second one put-to to dredge a different lane just outside the one the leader was working. When the third smack put-to she dredged a lane in the centre of the channel, while the fourth and fifth dredged the appropriate lanes over on the far side. Meanwhile the two leaders had finished towing and were beating back to complete the circle.

Watching the scene I began to realize that my first assessment had been too simple. The five smacks were not all behaving in the same way; I could see that the third, fourth and fifth ones had different problems from the other two. Being well out from the near shore when they finished towing they had to make an extra tack in before they could wend and pick up the circuit of five tacks made by the two leaders, yet somehow they were still keeping station. Each of these three smacks must be robbing nearly two minutes from somewhere.

For the moment the problem of the missing time defeated me, and I checked that the three smacks on the far side were not towing short. They were towing full length, so that was not the answer. The solution must be that they were towing faster than the two leaders and making time up this way. As soon as this occurred to me I could see at once that this was what they were doing. The two on the near side were towing with the peak run fully down, the staysail a'weather and the jib drawing, but the other three were not dropping so much peak and, in addition to having their staysails aback also had their jibs sheeted slightly to weather. They had more canvas working during the tow and were indeed towing appreciably faster than the two leaders.

That was fair enough, but the need for the extra tack meant that the last three smacks were ending their tows in quite a different way from the others and, watching, I saw that the difference was the order in which the dredges were hauled.

All the smacks were working four dredges evenly spaced down the length of the weather rail. The depth of water in the river was about two fathoms, so the dredges were towing on about six or eight fathoms of warp.

On the two leading smacks, the after dredge was hauled first, and the others in sequence going forwards, with about half a warp length delay between each. The timing of the other activities on board was meshed in with this.

At the end of the tow the skipper began hauling the after dredge, and at the same moment the man on the fore-deck began setting up the peak. By the time the skipper had his dredge at the rail and was lifting the bag inboard, the dredgerman next to him was lifting his dredge clear of the bottom. The smack was thus freed from the pull of her dredges aft and at the same time was beginning to feel the leeward pull of her peak. As a result she began luffing up to wind.

By the time the third dredgerman was lifting his dredge clear of the bottom the second man had brought his inboard and was free to move forward to let the staysail draw. Mean-time the man on the foredeck had begun hauling and the pull of his dredge brought the smack's head through the wind's eye so that in effect pull of this dredge had been used to wend the smack direct from the hove-to position.

On the other three smacks, which needed to make the extra tack, it was again the skipper who began hauling first, but he was followed at once by the man on the foredeck, while the other two men in the waist delayed by about half the length of a dredge warp. The skipper and the man on the foredeck thus had their dredges inboard while the other two were still hauling and had not yet lifted their dredges clear. As soon as the skipper had stowed his dredge he brought the smack's helm up and began steering, and a moment later the man on the foredeck let the staysail draw and then set up the peak. While he was doing this the two men amidships had finished hauling and moved forward, one to tend the jib, and the other to put the staysail on its bowline. The smack had thus broken away from being hove-to, and was on the port tack sailing in towards the near shore where she would wend and take up her place in the five tack circuit.

As soon as the smack was sailing again the men went back to their dredges and began culling out the catch. Clad in sea-boots, guernseys and white canvas sunhats, the men, middle-aged and even elderly, seemed deliberately to make it look as though the smacks were sailing themselves while they culled oysters. Even the skippers were to all appearances far more interested in what their dredges had caught than they were in weaving the smacks though their intricate courses among their neighbours.

I cast my mind back to the time the smacks had been getting away and realized that from the word go there had been no hint of raggedness. None of the smacks had hung about at anchor waiting for the right moment to get away and I guessed that on board each of them the skipper had nodded to the men on the halyards and from then on each man had set his own speed either lagging or leading as he thought fit, acting as watchdog to the others.

Hervey and I beating up the river that morning had thought that just two of us meshing in together was a gloriously skilful game, but here I was watching five smacks sailing as one and, as I guessed it, not a word spoken though all of them were within close collision distance constantly.

The scene had all the colour and the richness of an oil-painting and, although no two of the smacks were quite the same, all were true to type. Taken together in the tracery of movement, they wove their patterns back and forth one between another as though in ritual round the *Charlotte*.

The details of the sailing caught me up and I sat trying to predict each small adjustment as it was needed. A touch of peak here, a touch of jib there, a warp shifted aft or forward, a dredge hauled early or a fraction late. A tack sailed free and shortened or a tack sailed close and stretched. Slight corrections constantly, but the main movement flowing smoothly. There were never less than two smacks beating and never more than three, and always, if one smack were on one tack, her sisters would be on the same tack with her, perfectly in station.

For an hour they dredged with time unheeded but then the leader reached the end of her tow and without warning hauled her forward dredge first instead of last. She bore away instead of wending and as she went she set her peak. Each in turn the others followed, and the five smacks sailed silently away.

Reaching the bend lower down the river each rounded it gracefully and drew away behind the point. For a short time longer the heads of their sails still topped the far seawall, evenly spaced and thrusting forwards, but then as they turned into the next reach the spaces between them closed and one by one they dropped away below the skyline.

Only the *Charlotte* still remained and I saw that Hervey had come on deck. He waved to me and jumped into the dinghy to scull over and pick me up. I roused myself and walked down to meet him.

He was full of the incident which he had watched from closer range, and as the smacks had passed and repassed the *Charlotte* the crews had chaffed and talked, chiding him for not joining in and helping.

We pictured them bundling into their boats to go ashore, each to make his own way homeward and, for all the hardships of the winter, envied them for what seemed to be in so many ways an idyllic way to earn a living. Neither of us realized that not until that morning had we learned to understand the perfection we had just been watching.

Chapter 12

Hervey was tolerant about the smack verus barge argument and looking back on all those discussions now I think we were about evenly matched. Both barges and smacks possess the same kind of genuineness. The same appeal of colour, skill and grace to offset the drab facts of a livelihood that was hard won, but was real in a sense we could not quite define. In some ways both types of vessel caught the essence of the *esse quam videre* argument and we were both at an age when such things are important.

Out of our discussions came the suggestion that we would both forego the *Charlotte* for one weekend and make a barge trip to London River on different barges and then swap notes afterwards and compare our impressions.

Joshua Francis, of the Colchester firm Francis and Gilders, kindly agreed to this and arranged that just after Coronation Day Hervey and I were each to join a barge at Colchester and make the trip to London Docks. I was to go on the *Leslie West* with Joe Mumford as skipper and Hervey was to go on another barge, which I think was the *George Smeed*.

Hervey took me down to the barge-yard to meet Mr Mumford, who asked me to call him Joe and he would call me Michael. He was a slightly-built elderly man with white hair and was gently-spoken. At first glance it hardly seemed possible that such a man should from choice earn his living sailing a Thames barge in the winter gales of a treacherous estuary, but conflicting with this impression was a look of boyish excitement about his face as he schemed out a plan of campaign. He was quite firm that it would be almost pointless for me to ship merely as a third hand and proposed that, if it were possible for me, he would give his mate a week's holiday so that I could ship on board as temporary mate.

This needed some thought as, although my student duties were not arduous, I could not take a whole week off and expect to get away with it. On the other hand, the hospital was very near to the dock area, and given energy I thought I could satisfy both requirements. He was happy about this and pointed out that during most of the time a barge is in dock her crew can be ashore if they wish and in any case if it came to it he could easily manage the barge without a mate.

This seemed satisfactory and we arranged that I would telephone Francis and Gilders during the week to find out when the *Leslie West* was due to leave.

On our way back from the yard Hervey told me rather more about the *Leslie West* and her skipper. Joe had sailed for several years with his only son as mate and the boy had proved very apt. He had been given a barge of his own after the usual period as mate and had sailed her successfully for a period, but then during a winter gale the barge had dragged her anchor at night from where she had been brought up just below Southend Pier. She dragged out into the estuary and foundered. Both the boy and his mate were lost and after this Joe had retired more into himself. Increasingly he had taken to reading the Bible and was well known for this habit down the length of London River. He was respected by all the bargemen as a skipper who consistently made fast passages in weather which kept most of the barges swinging at their anchors. He averaged one round trip a week over the year, which was a record few skippers could rival. The *Leslie West* was one of the middle-size barges and was not by any means a fast one, but Joe had invested his savings in buying a share in her and had no wish to be transferred to a better and more profitable barge. The fact that in his hands the barge was able to beat most of the others had led to Joe having the reputation of being a noteable 'cracker-on', and recalling the look of lively interest in his face I could easily believe that he lived up to his reputation.

I joined the barge on the Thursday at about midday. She was lying against the Rowhedge Sand Ballast Quay and was already loaded, but the shore-gang were still putting the finishing touches to trimming the cargo. When they were done I helped Joe place the hatch-boards, and then batten down the covers, and we then set the topsail and staysail. There was very little wind, and a small tug appeared to give us a pluck away from the quay, and then swing the barge round to head away down Colne.

After we were round we let the brails down and sheeted the mainsail, and I then set the topmast staysail. Even in the light wind I found the single sheet difficult to harden in and Joe was beside me in a moment. Exerting far more strength than I had been able to, he had it sheeted home in one pull and then belayed it. With that he was gone, but called to me over his shoulder that the brake on the wheel was not working so he had to hurry.

Just below Wivenhoe the wind died and for nearly two hours we were becalmed. I scrubbed the decks down, and re-coiled the warps which had been shifted off the hatches during loading and then went aft to sit and yarn with Joe. My gear was still lying beside the cabin hatchway and he suggested that I should take it below and stow it somewhere on the port side, which was to be my side of the cabin. I had come in seaboots and blue sweater, but had brought with me my student clothes in which I could go back to the hospital if need be.

I had also brought a food stake and choosing what to bring

had not been very easy. I knew that the bargemen were reputed to live modestly but well and I thought that my usual *Charlotte* diet would not be very suitable. I decided to spend part of my savings buying a ham, which proved to be very good and was a good choice. In addition I had brought bread and various other oddments.

Hervey was to leave from Colchester Hythe on the same tide, but his barge would be sailing light and would thus have the advantage. There had been no talk of making the trip a race simply because Hervey and I were on board the two barges and I am sure that Joe would have sailed the *Leslie West* in the same way in any case. Even so our presence put an edge on the usual rivalry and one of the things which I most enjoyed about the trip was the opportunity of watching him use small factors to such advantage that he was able to build up a decisive lead.

We made slow sailing down Colne and in the distance astern Hervey's topsail seemed to be catching up a trifle. I had half expected Joe to bring up at Brightlingsea, but he made no sign of doing so and we continued ghosting slowly in light airs until we were at the extreme end of Colne Point by about slack water. Here we brought up, as there was no chance of stemming the flood down to the Spitway. I noticed that Hervey's barge had brought up off the entrance to Brightlingsea Creek. We had supper and then as it came dusk put up the riding light and turned in.

Joe woke me just before three o'clock. We had a quick breakfast and then turned out to get the barge away. There was still almost no wind, but we set the sails to a light draught from about west and drifted silently out towards the Bar. Joe took the inside swatch, but in fact had little alternative, as there was not enough wind to hold us up over the ebb. We half drifted and half sailed down to the Priory Spit and there the wind died to leave us becalmed. Joe brailed the mainsail and we set to work with sweeps to make our southing over to the Spitway.

The sweeps did not at first seem to have any effect on the deeply-laden barge, but slowly she did begin to gather way and after about half an hour of strenuous exercise we had her moving through the water at an appreciable speed. We gradually crept across the Wallet, but were still several hundred yards to the north of the Spitway buoy when the tide took us down to level with it. Joe was not concerned about this, and said that in due course the flood tide would sweep us through if we were far enough over to be in the right tide-lane. He pointed out to me the 'smooth' that we must cross in order to do this.

Not long afterwards we reached the smooth and Joe said I could stop using the sweep as the barge was now in soundings. I could begin 'poking her across' which was much easier work. Sure enough when I put the pole over we were in about two fathoms of water which quickly shoaled as I poled her in. We were by now well down on the Gunfleet side of the buoy, but poling her along was easy enough and we headed the barge up so that we were standing against the ebb as well as moving in over the sand. The soundings steadily decreased and after a time Joe said that we would be lucky if we managed to get over. Sure enough, soon after he had said this the barge gently took the ground and came to a stop.

Joe was a bit disappointed about this and said ruefully that he had not really expected to go ashore there. He concluded that the Spitway was steadily moving towards the west. This I think was said partly in defence and partly as being easier than trying to explain all that was in his mind, but in fact I could see well enough that the far tide-lane on the Swin side was worth about twelve hours if it stayed calm, and he was not being unreasonable to chance a grounding in order to get the barge as close as possible before the flood began running. We were already far enough over to be more or less clear of the Swire Hole tide and should easily be able to pole the barge the two or three hundred yards needed to get her over and away with a fair tide. While we waited we had a light meal of sandwiches and coffee.

When the first of the flood came it quickly floated the barge and, helping her with the poles, we were soon over to the deep water of the Swin. We now let the brails down and sheeted the mainsail to be ready for any wind which came to help us. A light breeze came up from just south of west, the barge picked up way and was soon moving steadily through the water.

Joe pointed out to me the wrecks which we passed and gave me the history of each of them. Nearly all were the wrecks of sailing barges, but some were older than living memory and he told me that the sands always 'gave up their wrecks' in June. Nearly all the very old wrecks were covered with sand during the winter months, but about June time each year they partly uncovered for a few weeks. It was quite regular every year and it always had been so, but he did not know the reason for it.

Some of the wrecks still had their masts and standing rigging and looked grimly forlorn. He told me that within a few hours of a crew abandoning a barge the fishermen stripped her of all that could be easily removed. He thought that it was odd that they found new wrecks so quickly when usually there were very few fishing boats in sight.

After we were past the Maplin Spit he gave me the helm and went off below to do his reading. The breeze was fresh by now and for about an hour I had the barge to manage single-handed and thoroughly enjoyed it. I was not fully happy with the wheel-steering and wished I could have sailed her with a tiller, though I knew that the bargemen had been grateful when the wheels had come in to replace the tillers with which steering had been a difficult and arduous business. Even so the barge was handling like a dinghy and in that weight of wind would have been marvellously good fun to sail with a tiller.

I found the long Francis and Gilders bob a difficult guide as to where the wind was coming from, as it seemed to lie much more to leeward of the curving topsail-head than I thought it should. At the beginning I several times came near to getting the barge in irons, but after a time picked up the hang of it and began to do better. To my great delight the *Leslie West* began to take the occasional sea over her bows and this I thought really was something.

Joe came on deck again when we were off the Shoebury buoys and as we were now approaching the main channels of commerce there was a score or more of barges in sight, some near and some more topsails on the horizon. I commented on this because even in those days we were beginning to mood about the dying out of the Thames barges. Joe told me that not long ago it had been usual to see sixty or seventy barges in sight down in this part of the estuary.

He looked round and began naming the barges easily and without hesitation and I quizzed him as to how he could be so sure. He laughed and said that a good many things entered into it.

Perhaps most important was the topsail and, listening to him talking, I began to realize that he probably knew the life history of almost every topsail in the river. He pointed out to me that an occasional one would be new and untanned, while others such as that one over there were freshly tanned and a different colour to the mainsail, but others were old and darkened compared with the mainsail which was newer. Some were patched and some were borrowed and did not fit the spars of the barge now using them. Quite apart from these things each class of barge had its own distinctive cut of topsail. That one with a flat head belonged to one of the iron-hulled barges, while the higher-headed one beyond her showed that the barge was one of the faster of the coastal barges.

He said that much depended on knowing where each barge was likely to be and which ones were likely to be sailing in which direction, and again, the position of a barge at a given state of tide could convey a lot. The iron barge was relying on the wind holding until the ebb set down, which in itself gave a lot of information, because each skipper nearly always behaved in the same way, though they differed greatly one between another.

I gathered that if I had given him a description of a barge and her course and position, even as seen through my unperceptive eyes, he could have said with tolerable certainty which barge it was and, when he added to that his keen perception of detail, the matter was clinched.

He pointed out to me that two of the more distant barges were ketches which I had failed to notice, though when he pointed it out it was clear enough. Another barge had a new bob which she had not had last time he saw her, but she had been needing a new one for some months. This I could not see and had to confess that his eyesight was better than mine. Later as the barge approached I could see that she did indeed have a new bob as he had spotted. Without difficulty he went round the horizon and gave a name to each barge in sight.

In the entrance to the Warp the wind took off to a light breeze and the tide turned so that we were sailing against the ebb. I had always heard that the bargemen worked their tides strictly and I expected Joe to bring up, but he made no sign of doing so. I tried to work this out, as we were beating now and making very slow progress.

We did not discuss the matter, but right or wrong, I worked it out that the *Leslie West* was laden and in light airs would be slower than Hervey's light barge behind us. If we were able to make over the ground beating up the Warp Hervey could certainly make ground over the ebb on his fetch down Swin. Both barges had to report for orders at Woolwich and the deadline for getting new orders would be early tomorrow morning. I guessed that Joe had it in mind first that there must be no chance given for Hervey to appear astern and then overtake us during the night, and beyond that I suspected that it would please him greatly if we could have received orders and be gone from Woolwich before the other barge arrived. I could easily enter into the spirit of this undeclared race.

During this part of the sail Joe sent me up forward with a boathook to spear likely lumps of firewood and I quickly gathered what seemed to me to be a pile of very good firewood, but after a time he left the barge to herself for a moment and came forward to look. He told me that most of what I had picked up would not do. With the choice they had available barge mates were fussy and only gathered clean wood of the right size and kind to chop easily and burn well. I went aft to take the helm while he sorted out my pile and threw most of it back. He then sent me forward again and by seeing which bits he had kept I had some guide as to what kinds now to begin collecting.

Soon after we passed Hole Haven it came dusk and we put the navigation lights up and continued beating. The flood tide was beginning to run and we began making better progress although the wind was still down to light airs. From this part on the river was new to me, but with the constant need to watch out for the lights of other vessels I was not able to study it very much. Simply, we sailed all night, tack and tack, dodging steamers and giving way as need be and I could only marvel at the quickness with which Joe was able to assess the significance of lights and distinguish between fast ocean-going vessels and the relatively slow river and coastal ones.

By the time daylight came the lights were beginning to tire me badly and I was glad to have ordinary vision back again to help. We carried the flood up to Woolwich and after brailing up gave the barge her anchor just short of a pair of dumb-barges. Joe had told me to give her a single scope of chain, but I underestimated the weight of the anchor and supposed it would behave in much the same way as the *Charlotte*'s. I fleeted the chain out freely and before I could check it, it had taken charge and another extra half scope had run out before I regained control of it. When the barge swung she was too near the lighters and caught her quarter a heavy blow across the bows of the nearest one.

I hove in chain as fast as I could and Joe came forward to help. The barge swung clear but she had a deep gash in her rubbing strake. Joe said there was no great harm done, but I was bitterly ashamed of my clumsy incompetence.

We finished the stowing of the sails and went below and after a brew of tea and a light meal I turned in at about six o'clock. With the exception of our short break while aground on the Gunfleet we had been at work for twenty-seven hours, and I could probably have slept the clock round, but sharp at eight o'clock Joe turned out without the aid of an alarm to wake him, and after he had prepared a quick breakfast I sculled him ashore to pick up orders.

Joe was dressed in his usual peaked cap, blue jacket and seaman's sweater, and looked smart enough to be on his way to an office job ashore. I was in sweater, slacks and seaboots, and probably looked a bit rough. The barge's boat was heavy to scull, but steady and, once moving, sculled quickly. I became aware that several other barges' boats were converging on the quay and began unobtrusively to race. Joe made no comment about this, but when I swept the boat round at the ladder I was well pleased at being the first to get there. He disappeared over the top of the quay, and for half an hour I waited together with a small cluster of other barges' boats. I found the mates friendly and easy to get along with and not curious about my background. Joe was the first skipper back. He climbed down the ladder and after he was in the boat I pushed off and sculled away towards the *Leslie West*.

When we were out of earshot he asked me humorously how I had made out with the other mates, and I had told him I had got along all right. He said that our orders were to go to Charlton Buoys and we would be leaving right away.

We set sail and beat up to Charlton where we found the tier of barges swung to the ebb. Joe brailed up half way across the river and then eased in. I ran down the topsail and staysail as we approached. He brought her alongside almost stationary against the tide, so gently that she barely rubbed. I stepped over the bows with a warp and made fast, while he made fast aft.

We then stowed the gear and went ashore to do the shopping. Joe gave me the money and put me in charge of this, but said I was to be sure to count the change. I did this and it was the first time in my life that I had ever done so. To my surprise I was short-changed in every shop we went to, and Joe told me that the cockneys always did this and probably always would. When the error was pointed out they made no argument about it but paid up with a purely casual apology. He told me it was not because they recognized me as a stranger, they did it to everyone.

Joe then took me to the bargemen's pub, and told me I would find most of the skippers and mates in the bar talking about barges, and it would be an experience for me to be among them and for the moment one of them. I realized then that he intended to wait outside until I returned and declined the offer. This amused him and I gathered that some of his mates had not been worried about keeping him waiting. We walked back to the landing place and went off on board. He went below to read while I lay on deck and dozed in the sun.

We turned in soon after dusk and I had a good night's sleep in the shut-off mate's bunk on the port side of the cabin. Both the skipper's and the mate's bunks ran aft from the cabin to the transom, one on each side, and were fully panelled in. Each was shut off from the cabin by a door and formed a kind of small bedroom on its own though there was only room to lie down in it.

On the Sunday morning we were up early and Joe set me the task of cooking breakfast on about eight small sticks of kindling wood. When he had done it there had been enough fire to do this and then boil the kettle again to do the washing up, but I made a poor fist of it, and had to use more wood so that the fire was still burning when I had finished. His fire had neatly gone out just as the kettle came to the boil. I admitted defeat, and he laughed and told me that given practice I would pick up the knack very quickly.

After breakfast I lit the kitchen range in the fo'c's'le and then scrubbed the decks. With that finished I went below and Joe asked me to wash all the cabin paint and varnish-work with warm soapy water. I then dried it thoroughly and gave it all a good polishing with furniture cream. Joe told me that the cabin, which looked as bright as if newly fitted out, had not been done for several years, and given this kind of care would continue to look new almost indefinitely.

Joe himself cooked the Sunday dinner, and I gathered that it was to be in the nature of a surprise. After finishing the cleaning I laid the cabin table with a clean cloth and put out the cutlery and so on. When the meal was ready, Joe carried it aft to the cabin on a dish under a metal cover. The dinner proved to be a round of roast beef with thick rich gravy, and on the same dish were piled roast and boiled potatoes, a sizeable cauliflower and a plum-duff which he told me had been boiling all the morning.

I was as hungry as a hunter and had two helpings of this

mixture, but he contented himself with a modest single portion. It was one of the tastiest meals I have ever eaten and the plum-duff with gravy was delicious.

During the afternoon I lounged on deck, and chatted to an elderly skipper whose barge had been on the buoy for some months while he was recovering from an operation which he had had in one of the teaching hospitals. He rebuked me for not addressing him as 'sir', as a skipper should be addressed and I remedied this. He was full of interesting reminiscences and the afternoon passed easily.

On the Monday we received orders for Waterloo Bridge, and sailed up to just short of Tower Bridge where we brought up and lowered the barge's gear. We then hove up anchor again and a friendly tug passed a warp to us and towed us to just beyond London Bridge. We towed alongside and I chatted with one of the tug's crew who told me that they invariably gave Joe a pluck if they were going in the same direction. I asked if this was routine for all sailing barges as I had been told that 'sailor-men' were highly respected on the river, but he told me not so. Holy Joe was in a special class of his own. I gathered from Joe afterwards that if a barge held up a warp a tug would always give her a tow if it were possible, but it would be charged to the owners. If the tug offered a tow it was 'on the house'.

The tug increased her speed just before she cast us off, and we carried our way right up to Waterloo Bridge where we brought up against a line of lighters. Joe landed me in my shore-going clothes, and I went home to Colchester for the night to have a good clean up. He would see to getting the barge into her dock by himself and would telephone to leave a message for me at the Porters' Lodge at the hospital to tell me when he was ready to come back down the river. He thought that this would probably be on the Wednesday.

I received his message on my arrival at the hospital on the Wednesday morning. I was to meet him at a dock just above Waterloo Bridge at about five o'clock. Giving myself plenty of time I set out to find him but it was easier said than done. I could see the *Leslie West*'s stern from half way across the bridge, but finding the dock in the maze of back-streets was much more difficult. I had a frustrating half hour asking various likely-looking people where the dock was. Eventually I found it for myself, and arrived only a few minutes late.

In fact there was plenty of time and the barge was not yet quite afloat. Joe was not intending to go down the river until the ebb was running strongly, and had thoughtfully said five o'clock only to avoid me having time to kill after finishing at the hospital. We went ashore together to do some shopping, but this time he took charge, and was not short-changed.

After the shopping we came back to the barge, and casting off the warps poled her out into the tideway. In dock the barges keep their anchors at the davit so that they do not run the risk of sitting on a fluke and being pricked, but out in the tideway the anchor is let down so that it hangs clear under the barge's bottom where it is out of harm's way during the many minor collisions which go on while she is lying on the tiers.

I was not aware of this, and after we had poled out did not follow something which Joe shouted to me as the tide caught the barge and began sweeping her up the river towards a tier of moored lighters. Quickly he came forward without further explanations and was just in time to lower the anchor clear before the barge fetched up against the tier. Even with a heavy wattle fender to break the impact she wrung appreciably as she struck and swung in to lie along-side. Fortunately Joe had been just in time clearing the anchor and no harm was done, but I began to realize just what a rough life a barge's hull is called on to put up with.

It was nearly dark before the tier swung to the ebb, but we hung on for another hour and then casting off wriggled our way out between the lighters which had come in after we had. The Waterloo Bridge tug slid crabwise across towards us. She took our warp and we lay alongside while she swung the barge round and gave us a pluck until we had good way on, after which she cast off. We carried our way down as far as Southwark Bridge, and then lowered the anchor a-trip to drive down. Below Tower Bridge we let out more chain and brought up to hoist the barge's gear. This was hard, slow work with both of us on the windlass and, in the darkness, I was not able to follow the details as closely as I would have wished. Eventually the work was all done and we set sail to run back down the river. Our orders were for Chalkstone Buoys, where we laid alongside the tier and brought up.

At seven o'clock next morning Joe woke me and gave me a good breakfast. I then collected up my things and he put me ashore. He took me up to the tram for Aldgate and from there I knew the way and could walk the rest. His mate was due back during the morning and my week crewing for him was over.

Afterwards we continued to see each other until the war came but then lost contact although Hervey from time to time gave me news of how Joe was getting on.

Some years after the war Hervey told me that the *Leslie West* had brought up inside Shore Ends at dusk during a winter gale and soon afterwards had begun to drag her anchor. In the nature of things dragging out into the Thames Estuary at night is the prelude to a foundering, and I knew that Joe, whose son had been lost after dragging had since then spent many hours working out how the predicament should best be met. The *Leslie West* foundered well in on the Foulness sands and it would be my guess that that in itself was a small epic of applied seamanship. Joe and his mate were able to take to the rigging where they spent the rest of the night safely though both suffered badly from exposure.

At dawn the barge came adry and they made their way across the flats to Foulness where Joe telephoned Joshua Francis. Josh came out from Colchester with a light barge and a crew of skippers. The cargo of wheat was sodden, but they were able to transfer enough of it for the *Leslie West* to float and she was sailed in. The wheat was dried and sold as cattle-food at a fairly good price, and 'the club' through which the barges are insured paid for the repairs. Joe and his mate fully recovered and took the barge over again to resume sailing.

Some years later Hervey told me that coming into Hey-bridge Basin with the wind aft Joe had eased the *Leslie West* in against the outside staithing, and the mate had jumped ashore with the warp to check the forward way. He had correctly hooked the splice over a bollard but unfortunately the warp-end was not securely made fast to the barge.

The *Leslie West* went through the lock gates, and since the club did not insure for damage to harbour installations Joe and Josh between them as joint owners had to pay for the repairs. The lock gates themselves were not too expensive, but one of the long wooden levers which topped the gates was sprung and had to be replaced. Originally the lever had been made from a rejected ship's kelson, and had cost almost nothing, but in the whole country there was not now another piece of pitch pine large enough to make a new one. The Court ruled that the new lever must be made of pitch pine, and they had had to pay for a baulk being felled in Canada and then shipped specially across the Atlantic. Joe had sold his house and his share in the barge, but even then Josh had to help him. Wisely perhaps he gave up sailing and retired.

Chapter 13

The *Teazer*'s log-book records that the trip on the *Leslie West* was first class, but I have not until now made any mention of the *Teazer* because she was at first only a side activity, although later she did play her part in the sequence which led to me becoming owner of the *Boadicea*. Her log-book has provided a good deal of the material for the earlier part of this tale and also for much of what follows.

Before talking about the *Teazer* herself I should say a few words about her log-book, because although I have found it a useful record as to facts, I have also found it irritatingly difficult to work from, and anyone reading these pages may perhaps profit from my mistakes.

The log is written in a school exercise book, which is fair enough. It records the day of the week faithfully and states the height of the barometer, the direction of the wind and what the weather was like. Hot fine days it dismisses briefly, but snow, storms and furious gales it records with approving detail, as also the fact that I was quite often wet and cold and tired, and almost always ravenously hungry. It often notes with satisfaction that I elected to miss the last bus home in favour of walking the eight or nine miles back to Colchester, and taken all round it is a vainglorious piece of boyhood writing. I take no exception to that because reading it again now I can still recall the incidents and seen through my eyes they were in fact pretty much as I described them.

The fault in the log is simply that during its entire length only two dates are mentioned, which is to say that it did not occur to me at that time that I would one day forget which month it was and which year, when such and such a thing took place.

Given a good deal of sleuthing I have been able to work out the months and years, but I would recommend to any youngster who sets out to keep a log that, unnecessary though it may seem at the time, he should begin each entry with the full date including the year. So much for the log-book, now let us turn to the *Teazer* herself, eighteen tons' displacement, registered at Maldon.

When I had first begun sailing in the *Bonito*, and later in the *Kestrel* and *Charlotte*, I had continued intermittently with the fastenings of the boat I was building at home. To put in the steamed frames I had shifted her outside and she was now on stocks under a chestnut tree in the garden.

Here on fine evenings it was pleasant enough to be working on her, and various of my friends had come down to help me because to do the fastenings properly two people are needed, one outside to hold the dolly on the nail-heads and one inside to set the roves.

Hervey had done his fair share of this work but, more clearly than I, realized that long before she was finished I would have already outgrown the boat, which would then be only an encumbrance.

He began to interest the Sea Scouts in the hull and when

they proved willing to take her persuaded me to let her go. This was a sensible move and freed me from a problem which I would not have solved very easily by myself.

This happened during the early part of the first winter when we were learning how to trawl on the *Charlotte*, and for several weeks the new activities fully occupied my spare energy, but soon after Christmas the thin ice coming down the creeks on still nights began to cut the smack's planking and we decided to shift her to be out of the tide. Feldy Creek had little flow of tide in it and was nearby so we put the *Charlotte* on a kedge and anchor just inside the entrance. This meant that she was afloat only for an hour or so each side of high water, but she was out of harm's way and yet could be easily brought out for sailing and fishing at the weekends.

I had not explored Feldy Creek and at once set about making good this omission. It is a short creek which runs in towards the seawall just above the Gut. When it reaches the seawall it turns to the north and peters out in a longish, narrow rill. In the main part of the creek there were two disused smack hulls which I examined closely. The nearest was called the *Firefly*. She was badly weathered and beyond all hope of further sailing. She was lying listing to port with her bows raised and, although empty of water, everything inside her hull was clothed in long strands of green clodge-weed, showing that the tide flowed freely through her.

She was not a very handsome smack and the line of her rails did not look natural. On further inspection I saw that she had been widened. About eighteen inches inboard of her rails her old covering-boards were incorporated in her deck and, looking below, I saw that the old planking still ran up to it. The parts on the outside were simply additional compartments, one on each side.

I pondered this and tried to work out whether the alteration to her shape had been the product of affection, or whether she had been used simply as a mule. Unwillingly, I thought most probably the latter. Either way she seemed past all hope and I went over to look at the second smack a few yards further inside the creek.

This one was quite different. She had shifted out of her dock and was listing heavily to starboard. She was called the *Teazer*. She was a big smack and was half full of water, but apart from that she seemed to me to be sound enough. Her deck was open from the sun, but the wood was hard and clean. Her topsides were badly open too, but again the wood was sound apart from one baddish area along her port sheerstrake. From the waterline down her seams were close and her planks were in better condition than the *Charlotte*'s. She still had her mast and standing rigging, and the mast had at its hounds a wide pair of cross-trees, which I studied critically. They were the same width as the deck and I took this as enough indication that this smack was a thoroughbred.

For a time I sat on her deck and thought about her and from there began thinking about boats in general. It was shortly after I had come to look on a vessel 'put-to' as being in what I called the fourth state of a boat, but now I began adding to this idea. The fifth state would be when a vessel was laid up and I thought about this.

When a boat is laid up she continues to have care and attention. In the winter she is safe in a mud-berth, but in summer the same berth will harm her and the sun falling each day on the same parts of her will quickly open her seams and sap at her vitality.

In summer she should be shifted out so that she can swing in the tideway, but she should come adry for at least half the tide to give her some protection underneath. If afloat all the time she will quickly grow barnacles, then green weed and shortly after that will begin to grow 'roses', as the fishermen call the highly-coloured little animals which grow quickly once the green weed is established.

Worm and roses go together and roses are a sign that mortal harm may already be begun. A yacht might be hauled out under cover to be laid up, but this was expensive and for working boats is usually an unattainable luxury. I thought about it all and decided that the critical quality of this fifth state was that the vessel needed attention and was receiving it.

The two smacks in Feldy had gone past that stage and were in a further one, a sixth state of being untended and laid aside to fend for themselves. I thought that the *Firefly* had been laid aside with no great regrets, but I felt sure that the *Teazer*, on whose decks I sat, had been laid aside with sadness and I guessed that she had been put into Feldy when her owner died.

I thought about this further and could understand that, according to her reputation and the demand for vessels of her type, any boat if she lives long enough will be obliged to face this sixth state with either confidence or hopelessness. If the period of fending for herself be short she will live, but if too long she will pine and die. The sixth state could quickly kill any boat though she had easily survived all other perils.

Beyond that there were other things. Only recently George V had died and had decreed that the *Britannia* should be shelled by the Fleet until she sank, and the harsh sentence had quelled the emotions of the whole nation. I had seen some of her sister 'J' class ships reduced to being houseboats and could easily sympathize with and endorse the harshness. These houseboats were in the seventh state, humbled and degraded. Some boats in this seventh state still sailed, or made a pretence of doing so, converted and improved upon, but they were stripped of their pride, and would have been better dead.

As the tide rose, I could hear from beneath her decks the soft musical note of water flowing through the *Teazer*'s open seams. She was filling quickly, but for a moment or two she lifted slightly. For some reason the movement appealed to me and I sat on until the rising water drove me from her deck. I had a long jump to reach the salting edge, but got across, and went back to the *Charlotte*.

The following weekend the weather was still hard, and we decided to leave the *Charlotte* where she was until the Sunday. At midnight I went over to the *Teazer* with a bucket as the tide left her and began to bail her out. I worked in

126

spells of fifty bucketfuls of water overboard for each stint, and then before going on again rested for about a minute.

By about six in the morning I had her empty and had a rest until daylight, when I went below and examined her frames and planking.

She seemed to be in sound condition, but as the tide returned she filled again and made only a slight movement before settling back. She still appealed and I went back to the *Charlotte* feeling that I had already formed some kind of bond with her.

The only real snag with her was her size. Being about eighteen tons she was too big for me to sail comfortably single-handed. We all accepted that although having a crew on board was pleasant, no boat was really suitable for our kind of sailing unless, at a pinch, she could be sailed and worked alone. Even barges could be sailed alone and one Wivenhoe skipper actually preferred to be without the worry of a mate. The *Teazer* would be a smaller undertaking than that, but was still too big to sail easily alone and do justice to her.

When I went back to the *Charlotte* Hervey and I talked about all this. He had a good deal of sympathy with my wish to try refloating her, but was worried about her size. From his visits to the barge-yard he knew that quite large shipwrighting jobs could be done without heavy outlay on equipment, and from helping me on the boat at home he knew that I was no botcher when it came to working on boats. He thought I could revive the *Teazer* without needing to spend more than the pocket-money I had, but was far less sure that she would be any good to me when I had done so.

Eventually we compromised and decided to offer five pounds for the hull, which was the limit of the money I could raise. If she could be bought for that amount I would go ahead, but if she would cost more than that to buy I would give up the idea.

When we went ashore we asked Sidney Hewes if he knew who owned her, and he told us that Hector Cook had laid her up in Feldy six years before when his father died and it was believed that he was determined that no one else should ever sail her.

We thought about this, and decided that it would be at least worth asking before giving up, and since I would be in London all the week Hervey said that if he could find the time he would go and see Hector Cook and find out what he thought of the idea.

Next weekend he told me that he had done this and had offered the five pounds. Mr Cook was not unattracted by the idea of trying to revive the *Teazer* but would like to think about it before making up his mind.

The following weekend he told me that he had been to inquire again, and had haggled a bargain which he thought would satisfy all concerned. Mr Cook was not unwilling for me to make the attempt, but had pointed out that although in the first instance he had been in the mind to lay the hull up complete for sentimental reasons, any decision to revive her put him in a different position. As executor he was bound to sell her for as much as she was worth. The hull itself was worth only five pounds perhaps, but the ballast could be sold at any time for twenty, and the mast as it stood was worth all of another five. Hervey had arranged that I would take the ballast out and ferry it across to Wyatt's where William Wyatt would buy it direct from Mr Cook, and meantime the mast could remain in the hull, but if I ever needed it I was to pay a further five pounds for it.

This arrangement appealed to Hervey's sense of humour, and he put it that getting the ballast out and ferrying it over the creek would at least keep me out of mischief for a month or two. I accepted the deal with delight, and during the next week took time off to go and see Mr Cook and paid over the five pounds. Incidentally it should be added that the extra five pounds for the mast was never charged. The *Teazer* of Maldon thus became my first command and somewhat full of my new importance I at once began her log-book.

Chapter 14

Before the deal had been completed the weather became milder again, and we laid the *Charlotte* off to lie afloat, but in deference to my activities Hervey put her on a mooring in the Gut where she would be near at hand to act as a base while I was making the attempt to refloat the *Teazer*.

I had no dinghy of my own and it would have been quite unfair to have used Hervey's dinghy to ferry the rusty pigs of ballast over the creek. William Wyatt was accommodating about this and told me that I could borrow the firm's hack-boat which would not be in use over the weekends in any case. I could use her for an hour either side of high water, and ferry the ballast over to the firm's slipway where I could unload it for his men to bring up to the store on the Monday.

The *Charlotte*'s weekend trawling was too interesting to miss, but my student duties were not very arduous and I easily arranged to get away early on Fridays so that I could go down and put in a good night's work before joining Hervey on the *Charlotte* at high water on the Saturday.

My method was to go over to the *Teazer* as soon as the tide began leaving her and start bailing right away. Given steady work I could have her dry in just under five hours, after which I began shifting ballast up to her deck. This part of the work was slow however, as the pigs were a hundred-weight each and were solidly rusted together. I soon discovered that in addition to a crow-bar, a cold chisel and heavy hammer were necessary parts of my equipment. I also took over a stout wood box which I could stand on for the final lift of each pig up to the deck.

The hull was swarming with crabs and judging by their size most of them must have been inhabitants ever since the smack had first sunk.

Working among the muddy pigs at night by the light of a hurricane lamp I found the crabs rather uncomfortable companions and foolishly killed any that I came across, which of course attracted hundreds more on the following tide quite apart from making the bilge smell abominably.

As soon as the returning tide began to flow in through the smack's seams I would give up working on the ballast and take Hervey's dinghy over the creek to collect the hack-boat. Leaving his dingy on the hack-boat's mooring I would then scull back to the *Teazer* and begin transferring the pile of pigs from the smack's deck to the hack-boat, and if I worked quickly would just have time to do this before the rising tide drove me off the smack's deck. The need for working quickly was now over and I could take my time to ferry the ballast over to the slipway and unload.

Usually, I would then leave the hack-boat beside the slip while I walked up to the sweetshop by Gowen's to buy my self a bar of chocolate which I would eat while sheltering in the lee of the sheds. After that I would lay the hack-boat off and go back to the *Charlotte* to have a meal and a rest.

After about six weekends of this routine there was an unusually high tide, and while I was standing eating my bar of chocolate one of the fishermen coming down the road gave me a grin and said, 'Whoa ho, she floats.' I followed the direction of his glance and to my surprise there the *Teazer* was. Only her deck and rails were above water, but she was on an even keel and undeniably afloat. He told me I should hurry back and try to shift her so that she would dry out in a new berth where she would sit upright.

I could still hardly believe that the *Teazer* really had floated but I needed no second bidding to row back to her as quickly as I could. When I reached her the water in her open hold hatch was almost level with the deck but she was still afloat and I shortened in her starboard chains both fore and aft by about a fathom. By now the tide had turned and I was only just in time. She took the ground almost immediately after I had shifted her.

To my delight, when she came adry she did sit upright, but was much slower in losing the water inside her as the only bad leaks had been along the covering board and sheer-strake. Going round her in the dinghy as she came adry I could see that although still three-quarters full very little water was leaking out of her. This was better than I had dared hope for, though it meant that I now had a great deal more water than usual to bail out. On the credit side was the fact that being upright she was much easier to bail than she had been when listing at forty-five degrees. I set to at once and made good progress.

Hervey was busy in Colchester and would not be down until dusk, and by the time I saw him at the causeway-end I had the water inside the smack down nearly to the level of the hold floor. I went over the creek to fetch him and found him nearly as excited as I was. He had noticed that the *Teazer*'s mast was upright the moment he arrived and realized at once that she must have floated.

We went back to her together and finished the bailing out fairly quickly. There was now nothing more that we could do except wait and find out what happened on the next tide. We went back to the *Charlotte* and lit the fire which in the excitement of the afternoon I had forgotten to attend to. We had a meal and decided that as we could not start trawling until the ebb set down we would wait on the mooring until nearly high water, and before setting out go over to the *Teazer* to find out how much she had leaked.

When we turned out it was bright moonlight and even from the *Charlotte*'s deck it was obvious that the *Teazer* was floating high in the water. We sculled over to her and to our delight found that she had barely leaked at all.

This was a great advance, and now that she floated each tide I would be free from the long periods of bailing each time that I went over to work on her. Even more important I could now work on her at any state of tide and would not need to miss quite so much sleep working at inconvenient times of night. My Easter vacation was just starting and I would be able to use all of it effectively.

The *Bonito* was due to come out of her mud-berth that weekend, and we had arranged to put the *Charlotte* back on her mooring by the Packing Marsh so that Peter could use the one in the Gut. Very decently, he agreed to let me use her as a base during my holiday, which saved me a good deal of rowing. By the end of the holiday I had the rest of the ballast cleared out and the ferrying finished with.

I had intendeed to leave the two bulkheads in place but to scrap all the rest of the inside fittings. In the event I scrapped the bulkheads too, and this was a good decision though I arrived at it for trivial reasons. What happened was that a pair of rats invaded the smack, and after spending a good deal of time chasing them back and forth I decided to clear the hull out completely so as to leave them no cover at all. When she had been thus gutted out it was obvious that structurally she was in very good condition and had no bad frames at all.

Hervey meantime had enjoyed all this and regaled me with tales of a rat he had once had on the *Kestrel*. Eventually he had succeeded in starving it out and had heard it go overboard one evening. Before it gave up however it had badly gnawed several of the *Kestrel*'s frames, and he surmised that if the *Teazer*'s frames were as steeped in crab-juice as I claimed they were the rats would eat the lot before giving up. This thought worried me almost to distraction.

In the event, the rats did no damage at all. On the contrary they seemed remarkably tame and friendly and when, in the end, they did go I almost missed their company.

After the hull was stripped clear I thoroughly scrubbed her from stem to stern and, when she had dried, set to and scraped all the wood down clean. This took several weekends, but I was helped by having a period of cold, windy weather which dried the wood very well. I then gave the whole inside of the boat except the deck-head a flowing coat of boiling creosote.

At the time I was unaware that creosote is highly inflammable and did not realize that I must have come within an ace of setting the whole boat on fire. Nor did I realize how irritant creosote is to the skin and it was not until the job was done that I woke up to the fact that my face was swelling badly.

With the inside of the smack now clean and honest I next put in new bulkheads and followed this with new floor bearers and a new floor. Lockers and bunks were made from the offcuts and this all went well enough, but my next move was less satisfactory.

The deck-planking was sound, but the seams were open from the sun, and when it rained they leaked quite badly. I had never used a caulking iron, and had somehow come by the idea that caulking was a mysterious art which would be too difficult for me to master. Only later was I to find out that given moderate intelligence caulking and paying seams properly is far from difficult.

Lacking this knowledge I decided to temporize. Until such time as I could afford to have the smack caulked properly I would cover the deck with canvas. This was a botch job from the beginning, and although I did manage to stop the rain leaking through, the amount of work involved was quite out of proportion. With less effort and time than I spent on the canvas I could easily have caulked and payed the whole deck properly, and thus have been finished with it.

During this period of working I enjoyed the company of a pair of kingfishers which had made their home in the forehatch of the *Firefly*. Wagtails nesting on the smacks were common enough and were regarded as something of a joke since they usually indicated that the owner of the boat had not been working very regularly. Kingfishers were more unusual, and in fact this pair is the only one I have ever seen working over salt water.

They seemed to do very well and quite often brought back good-sized fish to consume at leisure, but one weekend I missed them and went over to the *Firefly* to look in her hatchway half expecting to find that rats from the seawall had rifled their nest. To my sorrow I found both birds still inside, presumably drowned on a larger than usual night tide. I half-hoped that perhaps a new pair would appear in due course and took the precaution of taking out one board of the curved hatch so that it could not again act as a trap, but in fact no other birds did come. Charlie Hewes told me that Feldy was known to be a haunt of kingfishers, but as far as I know those two were the last of them.

On Charlie's advice I looted a discarded smack's stove from the tail of the Middle Ooze, and as he predicted found that it was undamaged and fully serviceable. When this was installed the evenings on board were much more comfortable, and having it lit each weekend helped to keep the smack well-aired and fresh inside.

During the summer holiday I stripped out the bad sheer-strake on the port side, and with a good deal of helpful advice from Wyatt's made a template for a new one. This I took over to the yard where they cut me out the new plank in inch and a half larch. This I planed up and ferried back to the smack.

Single-handed I found that the long plank was difficult to manage, but by using a system of guys and props did contrive to hold it in place while I bolted the after end home. With that done the length of the plank made it fairly easy to bend it into place down the smack's side fastening each station as I went forward.

When this was done there was no alternative but to try my hand at caulking and I bought myself a caulking iron and a ball of oakum. I found that although the oakum was fairly difficult to spin, the rest of the caulking was easy enough for the lower seam, though almost impossibly difficult to do adequately on the upper seam between the sheer-strake and the covering board.

I thus found out at first hand why this seam is called the 'devil', and largely it was because of this experience that twenty-five years later when I put in the *Boadicea*'s new covering boards I decided to use two and a half inch oak rebated to take the sheerstrakes and by this means managed to take most of the spite out of the 'devil'.

Having caulked round the new plank successfully I carried on and recaulked the rest of the top-sides without difficulty. The worst part of reviving the *Teazer* was now done and I began to take things more easily. The smack was dry and habitable and, being situated on the far side of the creek, she was well placed for anyone who was not averse to spending part of his time well away from urban life.

Each weekend I crewed on the *Charlotte* in the ordinary course, but when we came ashore I did not come home straight away, but instead borrowed the dinghy and went back over the creek to light a fire on board the *Teazer* and do various jobs until about midnight, when I would pack up and come ashore again to make my way back to Colchester on foot.

Usually to do this I took a short cut round to the Strood along the seawall, but to my surprise several people in the Victory warned me off and vaguely told me that the Strood seawall was not a healthy place to be after dark. At face value this looked like superstition, and there were several well-known tales of both the Strood causeway and the seawall being haunted. In fact I was not convinced.

Nearly everyone in Mersea was in bed by midnight and, during my walks I had not seen anyone about, yet someone must have seen me and I was more than slightly intrigued. I decided to be rather more circumspect in future, and took the trouble to do some exploring in the area of the Strood saltings, but beyond finding an apparently useless hedged-in lane I found nothing to support my hopeful ideas that perhaps contraband running was still a going concern.

During my late-night walks home I noticed that, in all the cottages I passed, a dim light had been left burning in one of the upstairs rooms, and at first wondered whether this could be put down to superstition, but later found out at first hand that oil-lamps have the disadvantage that they cannot always be quickly lit if light is needed urgently. It was a useful lesson and we learned it in a way which neither Hervey nor I are very likely to forget.

After a roughish January afternoon trawling in the Wallet we sailed the *Charlotte* into Harwich as it came dusk and decided to bring up well inshore in Harwich Pound. To do this we simply eased the smack in until she took the ground and then let the anchor down to rest on the mud beneath her fore-foot. Rather than pile the chain on top of the anchor we cleared it on deck and supposed that when the smack floated the weight of the anchor would draw the chain out.

This was a slipshod way of thinking and we certainly should have realized that there was a good chance of the chain fouling in the davit so that when the smack floated she would pick up her anchor and go adrift.

Since we had brought up well clear of the fairway we decided against putting out a riding light and when we turned in we blew out the cabin lamp.

Just before midnight we were woken by the sound of something heavy grinding alongside, and turned out to find that the *Charlotte* had drifted across the fairway and was beside one of the laid up lightships on the Shotley shore. We pushed her clear, and with the two of us sculling began to work back towards Harwich Pound. We were still not fully awake, but now realized that the lights we could see up-river from us were on the move, and that in fact the much advertised Harwich Night Parade of five packet boats in line ahead had just set out from Parkestone Quay.

Hervey sent me below to light the riding light, but in the blackness of the unlit cabin I was unable to put my hands on a box of matches. After about two minutes of searching Hervey called to me urgently to come on deck in case the smack should be run down and I came up to find that the first of the packets was about fifty yards away and seemed likely to pass with about thirty yards clearance. Seen from that range her bow-wave was impressive.

Adrift on a dark night in the centre of Harwich fairway without a single light on board we were not in a position to be critical, and after the five packets had gone past without any of them hitting us we were curious as to whether they had seen us and deliberately taught us a lesson we were not likely to forget or whether possibly none of them had seen the smack at all. We decided that if the five helmsmen had seen us they had certainly made the most of their opportunities.

In subdued mood we sculled the *Charlotte* back to the shallows and then brought up again, but this time made quite sure that the anchor was holding before we went below. When we turned in this time we did not blow out the lamp, but merely turned it down to burn less brightly.

Chapter 15

When the *Teazer* had first floated she was very nearly water-tight, but gradually began to leak unpredictably and I deduced that somewhere underneath there was a seam which had lost its caulking and was now filled with mud which occasionally washed out. While the mud was in place all was well, but if it washed out she leaked seriously.

I should have done something about this and did consider putting her on the hard to go over her lower seams, but was scared of her taking charge while among other boats and possibly doing more damage than I could pay for. I procrastinated and accepted the occasional bouts of heavy pumping out without complaint.

This continued until the autumn and then without warning she sank during a single tide. This time the bailing out took over twelve hours because, with her top-sides caulked, none of the water could run out of her. When the bailing was finished I had the depressing job of clearing up the mess below decks and this certainly should have warned me that something serious was wrong and needed to be put right. In fact she then stopped leaking altogether for a time and too easily I was led to procrastinate again.

Meanwhile Charlie had found me an old gaff and a boom from behind 'the back of Sid's' and these I planed up and floated over to Feldy. Hervey found a suit of secondhand sails at Wivenhoe which Lewis Worsp sold to me at the concessional price of two pounds and, thus equipped, I now began to look on the *Teazer* as virtually seaworthy.

During the period of the ballast-shifting and creosoting I had come to be called 'Darty-face' in the Victory, but now this changed to 'Gybe-ho', which I thought was a distinct improvement. Partly it was this I think which led me into taking the smack out on a quite unpremeditated sail.

Originally the idea was simply that I should shift her a few yards nearer to the mouth of Feldy Creek in order to get clear of the quagmire I had trodden up during my constant comings and goings over the saltings. To do this I had to raise her four anchors, all of which were so large that I could barely move them and, having shifted, I would then have to lay the anchors out again to remoor her.

This I had decided but, having once got the anchors on board, the opportunity of being free was too good to miss and on the spur of the moment I set up a jury mainsail in addition to the jib which I had intended using to make the move. This was done while I was waiting for her to float, and then when she finally lifted I gaily sailed away out into Ray Creek without any real plan about what I intended doing next. The wind was westerly, and on a broad reach I sailed up Ray watching the saltings cover without any worries. The smack was sailing beautifully and it was only when the last of the saltings had covered that I realized that I was now at sea in a featureless expanse of water and liable at any moment to run ashore on the salting edge. I turned off into Sampson's Creek and dropped an anchor.

When the tide ebbed I decided that rather than take her back to Feldy and moor all-fours again I would put out a second anchor where she was and let her swing between them. This was easily done and afterwards I rowed back down Ray thinking that the smack looked much healthier out in the open.

In many ways this unplanned sail was foolish, but it did also have some usefulness, and not least was the fact that she was now too far away to be quickly reached which made it much easier for me to neglect her. At that time I was getting very near to taking my final exams and urgently needed to begin studying in earnest. The new berth in Sampson's Creek gave me the opportunity to do this without any great pangs of conscience. Also the move resulted indirectly in the *Teazer* acquiring a dinghy and this had far-reaching effects which no one could have predicted.

The difficulty of getting to the *Teazer* in her new berth was not only one of distance. I had no dinghy of my own, but while she was lying in Feldy I was in sight of the causeway, and could thus easily borrow either the *Charlotte*'s or the *Bonito*'s dinghy and then keep an eye on the hard so as to row across and hand the dinghy over as soon as the others came down.

Occasionally I would be below and miss them when they arrived, but when this happened they would borrow a boat and come over to rouse me, and usually spent a few minutes on board either helping or hindering according to which mood took them. The first sign that I had missed them would normally be that the fire began smoking badly, and I soon discovered that this meant that one of them had crept on board unobserved and stuffed a lump of salting grass down the chimney. Given this kind of ragging my dinghy borrowing did not seem to upset anyone very much.

Sampson's Creek was a different matter however and it was obvious that I must now find some other way of getting to her. In the event I took to hiring Sidney Hewes's *Colne* for the morning about each fortnight, and doing this had a number of pleasant sails exploring creeks which were too far away to be easily reached by rowing.

On one such occasion I decided to sail up to the head of Ray which I had never visited, but soon after passing Ray Island the wind dropped and I anchored to wait until the ebb should set down and drift me back to the hard. I settled down to enjoy the sunshine while it lasted and was reasonably warm.

Meanwhile the saltings were beginning to cover and I noticed that a fox had stayed out too late and was now marooned on a maze of small salting islets. Unhurriedly, but still without wasting any time he was trotting back and forth down the length of whichever islet he was on until satisfied that there was no easy way off it. He would then make a leap to the next islet and repeat the sequence, and then similarly to the next islet again.

The water was by now lipping the surface of the islets, and each of his jumps brought him clearly in silhouette against the water beyond and with his long brush trailing he made a very striking spectacle. His trajectory was interesting, and the end part of his leap was always a vertical drop of about three feet. As the tide rose higher the edges of the islets began to cover and the length of his jumps increased. Also his pace was becoming quicker. Leap after leap, longer and yet longer, and the intervals between the leaps shorter. As a feat of endurance his performance was magnificent, but it could not last much longer, and in the end he tried a jump which was more than he could manage and he fell in. He climbed out on the far side and continued, but with his brush now wet he was badly handicapped, and as the tide continued to rise the length of the jumps became too long altogether. Repeatedly he fell in but still continued until at least all the patch of islets he was on covered. He gave up jumping and, swimming and walking, made his way over to a solitary patch of high grass which was still showing. There he sat on his haunches upright like a dog on guard.

The tide rose round him, but for some reason he made no attempt to swim back to Ray Island which was no more than a hundred yards away. When only his head and neck were still uncovered a pair of gulls began to mob him, but he snapped back viciously and screaming they kept just clear of his jaws. Other gulls joined in until a score or more of them were attacking him from all sides.

He could not hold out against this kind of odds indefinitely and I roused up and got the *Colne*'s anchor and began sculling in towards the salting edge. I had no intention of taking her in over the top unless the tide came a good deal higher, but from the edge I would be near enough that possibly the gulls would make away. If need be I could land and flounder across the covered saltings, but did not wish to get too near so as to scare him off his high patch into deeper water.

In the event my moving in did keep the gulls off him and the tide if anything was now beginning to ebb. For half an hour we sat and looked at each other. His glance was neither defiant nor unfriendly, but most certainly it was not defeated.

Gradually the tide receded and his body uncovered again, until he was sitting once more on his small island surrounded by shallow water. The saltings themselves now began to uncover, but he continued to sit on until finally the sunken causeway came adry. Then at last he made a move. Without a glance in my direction he stood up and shook himself and then, slightly dishevelled, but still carrying himself with an air of graceful nonchalance he loped away towards Peldon with an unhurriedness which I am quite sure was intended for my benefit.

The following weekend Sidney told me that the *Teazer* had sunk again and I borrowed one of his dinghies to row up to her and spent the rest of the day bailing out. This was thoroughly depressing, but I had her dry by Saturday evening and decided that I would leave her where she was until the following Wednesday when I would have two days off as some exams were going on. I decided that I would sail her down Ray to bring her over to the high soft mud on the Strood side of the No'the where I would moor her until my own exams were over.

High water on the Wednesday would be at about midday and I thought that if the wind should be northerly I could get away on the flood to make the whole passage in one tide, but if the wind should have much south in it my jury rig would not be good enough to beat her down Ray against the tide. In that case I would need to wait until the ebb was running well and then bring up on Ray Point to take her over to the No'the on the second tide.

In the event the wind was south-west and strong, and I got away at high water to make a long and short leg beat down Ray. On reaching Ray Point I thought that the tide was too far gone to be sure of getting in over the flat mud across the Strood and accordingly brought up to wait until the night tide. The smack lay over well when the tide left her and I took the opportunity of looking round her lower seams on the port side and found them all close and full, from which I concluded that the bad seam must be to starboard.

On the midnight tide I sailed her over to the No'the under jib alone making a cheating course against the first of the ebb. All went well until the last moment, and then a squall caught me unawares and the smack took charge.

She was well clear of any other boats and there was no possibility of her doing any harm. The crux of the thing was that it was so perversely inconvenient. Even now I cannot quite work out how she did it. One moment I was on the point of dropping an anchor exactly where I had intended, but before I could do anything to prevent her she luffed across the tide and drove herself hard ashore on the salting edge. Conceivably she was 'smelling the mud' aft and the tide swept her bows across, but at the time I thought she had been hopelessly perverse and felt thoroughly despondent.

The anchors were too heavy to manage from a dinghy, so I had no alternative but to wait until the mud uncovered when I dragged the lightest of them out so that on the next tide she would float clear. Before the squall the night had been fine but cold, but the squall had brought rain with it, and dragging the anchor out was not only unpleasant, but was far more difficult than I expected. When all was done I turned in on board and was glad to be under cover.

On the tide next morning I laid the second anchor and let her swing between them. She was now where I had first intended, and would float only for a short period even on the big tides. It seemed to me that she should be safe enough, but I came home feeling rather disappointed about the whole business.

Meanwhile Hervey had been looking round to find me a dinghy, and reported that two smack's boats were for sale at Rowhedge for five shillings each. This did not sound very promising, but we decided that it would be worth going round to have a look at them.

We did this and I was sorry to find that these were the boats of the two smacks which had shared the *Beryl's* mud-dock only a year or two before. Both smacks were now laid up and the men told us the usual tale of those days. Long periods of catching too few fish, and then when good catches were made the market glutted so that none could be sold at a fair price.

This was sad news indeed. The men recognized me from the *Beryl* days and we spent perhaps half an hour yarning with them. They were all working on shore and were far from happy, but had no alternative. They knew the two boats were precious little good, but had decided to try selling them before they dropped to pieces.

One of them had a moderately good top, but leaked badly and none of the shipwrights had been able to stop her. The other had her sheerstrakes stove-in, but was reasonably sound underneath and did not leak. I could take my pick and welcome. Sorry words for a man who is selling off his tools.

In the event we said that we would go back to Mersea and ask advice from William Wyatt. They agreed to this and it was arranged that I could take whichever I wished, and one of the men would be at the dock at midday on Saturday to help me push her down to the water.

William Wyatt had no doubts in the matter. Anyone could stop a smack's boat leaking if the top was good, but if the top was bad she was waffy right through. It was decided that I would take the leaky boat. Even at the time it seemed a slightly odd decision.

Collecting the dinghy was to be a combined operation. Since I was taking the leaky one the outside passage round Mersea would not be sensible, and instead I was to row her to Pyefleet, and then come round inside the island to the Strood causeway where Peter and Frank would meet me off the five o'clock bus. They would persuade the driver to stop the bus while they helped me drag the boat across the road and would then rejoin the bus while I carried on down Strood towards the hard.

On the Saturday morning Hervey ran me to Rowhedge with a set of rowing tholes and a pair of oars. I also took a bucket for bailing out as need be. We paid the five shillings and one of the men helped me push the leaky boat down to the water. The wind was south-westerly and fresh which was not helpful and I realized that I was in for a good hard pull if I was to be at the Strood in time.

I set out, and within the first hundred yards realized that I was in for more trouble than I had reckoned on. The boat griped badly even from the start when she was empty, but worse, she trimmed by the head so that any water in her ran forward to make her gripe even more.

During the whole row round I was pulling on first one oar and then on the other, but for almost none of the time was I able to pull both together. Long before I reached the mouth of Pyefleet I was worrying about not reaching the Strood in time, but fortunately was able to do rather better once I was round the point and had some lee from the salt-ings. By dint of pulling at full stretch I was very nearly in time, and was at least in sight when the bus reached the Strood. Very decently the driver waited for a full five min-utes while I rowed the last quarter of a mile.

Several of the passengers came out of the bus to help and as soon as the boat reached the wall, willing hands pulled her up to the road and then dragged her across to launch down on the other side. They pushed me off and then boarded the bus again. With much cheering and cat-calling the bus then drove off with no more delay.

The row down Strood was a less hurried one. The wind was beginning to take off which made things easier, and not being rowed so hard the dinghy neither leaked so quickly nor griped so much. Even so she was by no means behaving as I would have wished her to, and by the time I reached the *Teazer* I was not sorry to climb out of her to board the smack and make myself a very welcome brew of tea.

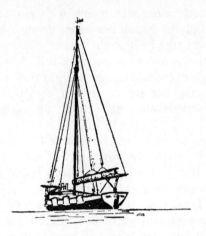

Chapter 16

By the time I reached the *Teazer* the tide was ebbing quickly and, since I had no wish to stay so long that I would have to push the new dinghy down across the flat mud, I sat on deck to drink my tea so that I could watch the tide and leave at the last moment.

The idea of possessing my own dinghy and no longer being a nuisance to other people was attractive, but the dinghy itself did not seem to be a subject for great gladness. On the way round she had not behaved at all well. The leaking could be forgiven and anyway that had been accepted from the start, but the griping was a different matter and it seemed to me that possibly she never would be any good.

Later, in discussion, William Wyatt brusquely told me that any fool should have known that a lump of cant-mud put in her stern-sheets would have made her behaviour as different again, but this knowledge was not mine, and sitting on the *Teazer*'s deck I felt vaguely despondent about the whole subject.

In parenthesis it should be said that some years later I

realized exactly what was wrong with her and could have cured it, simply by giving her wider thwarts, but that can be left over to emerge in its right place.

At the time, my reaction was that I would give her another chance. I would not go straight back to the *Charlotte* but would take her for a row out to Deeps and find out whether given leisure, she could be persuaded to row straight.

Just before the tide left the *Teazer* I boarded the dinghy again and set off for my row out to Deeps. The pull round from Colne had been a long one and I found that my hands were more sore than I had realized. The dinghy was leaking if anything faster than before and she seemed to be possessed by some wayward purpose of her own. No matter what I did with her she took her head and was away either to port or starboard without rhyme or reason.

By the time I was clearing the end of Mersea Fleet she was nearly half full of water and I continued only because I was unwilling to admit complete defeat.

At the inshore end of Deeps I tied up to the rigging of a smack and set to to bail out. To do this I sat on the dinghy's transom and bailed with the bucket and then, when she was dry, sat and looked at her from this vantage point. She was a typical Colne-built dinghy, with a weak narrow head and virtually no sheer. She looked seedy and tired of life, but I was tired myself and hoped that by the next morning the situation would seem less depressing.

I put her stern-sheets back in place and then stood up to glance at the smack I had tied up to. My painter was fast to her port rigging and I was lying alongside more or less amidships.

At different times I had looked at nearly every smack in Mersea and knew that, with one or two exceptions, they were all kept scrupulously tidy. I took tidiness for granted, but without ever really having thought about it. I also took it for granted that any working boat has a well-washed and even slightly threadbare look.

The smack I looked at now was certainly not threadbare.

As I had expected, the formal stowing of her gear was meticulous but beyond that there was something about her which put me in mind of a freshly-minted coin.

She had four dredges spaced down her deck, with their riggings draped outboard of the rail. Every other smack in Mersea carried her dredges in the same way but somehow without the same effect. I realized that the four dredges were new. One of them was beside me and I looked at it closely. The galvanizing on the wire riggings was bright, and even the cut ends of the wire rings were not yet tarnished. I counted the rings of the rigging. Fourteen across and seven deep and, unrusted as they were, they still tinkled softly as I moved them. The cotton netting of the dredge-back still had an unused whiteness and I counted the meshes, fourteen across and fourteen deep. The rawhide thongs were neatly cut to an even width and each was rove with the twists in it following through exactly as they should be. The set of the dredge was perfect. Whoever had rigged it most certainly knew his trade.

Beside each dredge a new bass warp was coiled, with its buoy attached to it. I realized that everything was new. The rails and decks were freshly painted, but beneath the paint they were quite unworn. The sails were flax and still untanned. They were obviously new. The spunyarn serving of the standing rigging was not yet discoloured and above the servings the wire was still brightly galvanized.

I was more than just intrigued by now. Newness in itself has no great appeal, but here newness was combined with motive, and none of the things I looked at had been merely bought. Each had been made with a kind regard to detail. I glanced at the rigging lanyards knowing what I sought and was not disappointed.

The dead-eyes had flowing convex curves and no flat surfaces. The lanyards were freshly dressed with Stockholm tar and the colour of the Italian hemp was richly alive. Each of the lanyards was set up as though intended as an object lesson on how rigging should properly be done. There was no question of finding fault. Each was a perfection in itself. Almost without thinking I stepped on board. I had occasionally boarded laid-up boats to look at them and this was almost permissible, but boarding a boat without good reason while she is in commission is next to piracy. I had never done this before and have never done it since. I do not fully understand what came over me to do it then.

She was lying wind-rode and was lifting to a slight swell. Without realizing, I gauged her motion and approved of it. I crossed her deck and felt her answer to the shift of weight and again assessed her movement and approved. I went aft and sat on her quarter and studied her from this position.

She was elusively familiar, but I could find no reason for it. She was short and her decks were very wide. They were well cambered and both fore and aft they ran up in a good bold sheer. She was nearly as round as an apple.

Her spars and blocks were bright varnished and all her rope was honey-coloured new. At her mast-head she flaunted a small golden chariot and a scarlet streamer. It was almost vainglorious, yet somehow it suited her exactly.

After a time I began to realize that I had no right to be sitting where I was and, as this fact dawned on me, I quickly recrossed her deck and dropped into the dinghy. For a few moments I stayed alongside, but then let the boat drift aft, and as I reached the smack's stern I read her name and port of registry. She was the *Boadicea*, but for a moment I was hardly able to believe it.

This was not the moment to be involved in struggling with the sorry little dinghy and, instead of rowing her, I sat aft on her gunwale and sculled as need be while the wind drifted me back up Thornfleet.

I was at first unable to believe the great change since I had last been on board of the *Boadicea*, but then recalled that some months before I had seen the hull of a small smack at the top of Wyatt's hard. She had her deck and bulwarks and topsides stripped away and I realized now that this must have been the *Boadicea*. Clearly Wyatt's had done their work well and clearly Manny French, who owned her, had spared no pains in fitting her out to work. I guessed that she was freshly laid off that afternoon to begin work on the coming Monday.

I was still concerned with having thoughtlessly stepped

on board of her, and knew that from on-shore the act would certainly have been observed. I knew too that the elder fishermen would certainly rebuke me when I met them next and I felt miserably sure that Manny would resent my intrusion. I decided to make a point of catching him as soon as possible to make my apologies.

In due course the wind drifted me back to the *Charlotte*, and I recounted to Hervey something of the incident. To my surprise he did not rag me about it, but told me seriously that the sooner I swapped the *Teazer* for the *Boadicea* the better it would please everybody.

This was a way of looking at the matter which had not occurred to me and even when thus put into words, it did not make any great impression. The *Boadicea* was Manny's and, although I envied him the good job he had made of her, it did not enter my mind to envy him his boat.

The new dinghy was still leaking badly and just before dark I bailed her out again, and then ferried her over the creek to put her on the hard. There later she filled and sat squarely on an anchor. She was not repaired and she never rowed again.

On the Sunday evening I chanced to meet Manny and told him that I had so much admired the *Boadicea* that I had not been able to resist stepping on board of her. By way of rounding off the apology I added that if he should ever think of parting with her I would very much like to have first offer.

This was banter and we both knew it, and he replied in the same vein that it had not been his intention to let just anybody have her. This was a fair reply and we both laughed and there the matter rested.

Chapter 17

Shortly after my boarding of the *Boadicea* we brought the *Charlotte* on the hard for a refit in readiness for making our first North Sea crossing. Since we looked on this as a yachting trip we put the trawl and dredges on shore and then repainted the hull. In addition, she was scrubbed and antifouled. This was completed in two weekends and by the time we laid her off again she looked tidy, workmanlike and, in our opinion, fit to mix in any company.

Our plan was to make for Holland direct and put in at either Flushing or the Roompot. This did not involve very much more sailing distance than making a channel crossing to Belgium, but the difference between the two undertakings was considerable. To be offered a Belgian cigar on board someone else's boat was almost nothing but a Dutch one demanded considerable respect.

These distinctions are now lost because almost all yachts carry barometers and wireless sets and have engines. Also holidays are usually longer now and in addition most owners nowadays would not be unduly concerned if rough weather obliged them to leave their boats over on the other side to be collected later.

From our point of view the hazards were the old-fashioned ones of calms and gales. On the Belgian crossing both could be avoided given reasonable judgement, but on the longer North Sea crossing there was at least an element of anxiety about the weather and also about getting the vessel back in the time available.

This latter consideration was in fact the more serious of the two, and our plan was to go as far as possible in the first third of the holiday, and then begin working back so that we could steadily reduce the length of the return crossing which would be made in unpredictable conditions.

It could perhaps be noted that not everyone adopted this plan and Archie White, who made as good passages as anybody, claimed that he always ran to leeward for the first week on the basis that the wind was very unlikely to hold from one direction for a whole fortnight.

Our immediate motive was not merely to go as far as possible in the time. Specifically we wished to go to Holland, partly because we had heard so much about its attractions, but also because we wished to provide the *Charlotte* with her own supply of Dutch cigars. None of us really admitted this second motive, but it was a very strong one for all of that.

To make the passage Hervey enlisted the help of Chaundy who was a student friend of mine. He had been down several times to help me on the *Teazer* and although he had not been on boats before had learned quickly. He had spent several roughish trawling trips on the *Charlotte*, and he and Hervey got along very well together.

We met on the causeway early on the Friday evening and loaded the dinghy with our supplies and gear. We then climbed in ourselves and found that the combined weight put the dinghy down nearly to her gunwales. Rowing carefully, we made the ferry trip out to the smack with no trouble and, after transferring the load, hauled the dinghy out on deck where we lashed it down securely. It was by now approaching high water and without further delay we set up sail and began our passage. We reached the North East Gunfleet just as it came dark.

The wind was moderate to fresh south-westerly and we made good sailing to the Galloper where the amount of sea running began to increase and, taking it on her weather quarter, the *Charlotte* picked up an uncomfortable corkscrew motion and needed a good deal of steering.

Hervey who was a martyr to seasickness was ill almost at once, but this we had all anticipated and, apart from feeling profoundly sorry for him, there was nothing we could do to help. We tried to persuade him to go below and turn in, but he declined to do this and continued to take the helm.

Despite her rather heavy rolling, the *Charlotte* was making good speed and by about an hour before dawn we had identified several of the lights wheeling below the horizon from the Belgian coast. This was encouraging and when dawn began to show we were all confident. Hervey now agreed to go below.

None of us was used to the North Sea and we did not appreciate that the Belgian lights were visible below the horizon long before land can be sighted and, when it came full daylight with no land visible, both Chaundy and I were unbelieving. We both knew that we were sailing nearly parallel with the coast and closing it only slowly, but it was disappointing that we could have been sailing so fast for so long without any sign of having made progress. Without any warning I was seasick and very soon after Chaundy followed suit. We agreed that this was psychological, but it was no more agreeable for that and for the next half hour we both felt thoroughly ill.

Meanwhile the wind was increasing and although we delayed, it soon became clear that something would carry away if we did not reef soon. A tramp steamer came past going in the opposite direction and although pitching slightly did not seem to be rolling at all. The *Charlotte*'s motion by now was lively to say the least of it and the contrast decided us. We hove-to to reef and eased the smack by running the peak half down and dowsing the jib.

After that we ran into trouble and the fault was entirely

mine. In furtherance of our yachting aspirations I had untied the bowlines in the hauling ends of the reef pennants and had replaced them with tidier-looking figure of eight knots so that there was no loop ready to take the reef tackle.

We tried to pull in enough slack by hand to retie the bowline but could not do it. In an attempt to reduce the weight on the sail we then started the throat halyard but, reacting to this, the smack which had before been hove-to comfortably, now bore away so that the mainsail was doubly full of wind. Clearly that would not do and we reset the throat.

Meanwhile Hervey had come on deck to find out what we were doing and with two hauling on the pennant we just managed to get enough slack for the third one to tie the bowline. It was a struggle for all that and we were lucky that no one went overboard in the process.

The rest of the reefing was now straightforward and a few minutes later we resumed course with the smack sailing much more easily under reduced canvas. Hervey went below again and with our morale improving we soon forgot our seasickness and had a light breakfast.

Later on, Chaundy who was doing the navigation announced that we had made our landfall, and gave me a course which brought the smack up close-hauled, and half an hour later we had Westkapelle abeam to port. From being alone in the emptiness of the North Sea we were now quickly in coastal waters with any number of small Dutch trawlers round us working under sail and we were all excited.

We locked in at Flushing soon after midday and lay beside the quay in the Middleburg Canal. We stowed the sails and tidied up and then made a short jaunt ashore to buy cigars. Even in the few minutes which this took, it was clear that Holland was every bit as good as we had been led to expect and we went back on board feeling tired but jubilant. Some hours later we woke to find the kettle boiled dry and our cigar butts lying on our chests.

In the evening we tidied ourselves and went ashore for our first proper look at Holland and we thoroughly approved of all we saw. The houses and the streets were noticeably clean and more than half the womenfolk were in national dress. Everybody seemed to be open-faced and in good spirits and the colourful throng was quite different from anything we had ever seen before.

We were impressed at finding two fishermen mending a sail spread out in the street regardless of the traffic which obligingly kept to one side to leave them undisturbed and this incident, perhaps as much as anything else, created for us an impression of a people who still put first things first. This impression was sustained and fortified at each new place we visited.

On the Sunday morning we again went ashore to do further exploring and for a time stood on the breakwater watching a contingent of Naval cadets man half a dozen whalers and row them out to sea. The wind was onshore causing a heavy swell which threw the flimsy-looking whalers about as the boys rowed off and quite often hid them altogether. The Flushing people lined the breakwater and watched silently, but with obvious pride.

With our tails slightly between our legs we commented that if our Navy had done the same thing in private they might have got away with it, but if they tried it in public the House of Commons would be up in arms and half the Sea Lords would resign for reasons quite unconnected with the incident.

We watched the boys until they were out of sight and then moved along to look at the boats in the fishing basin. We had passed any number of these boats on our way in the day before and now stopped to study them more closely.

They were all smallish wooden hulls with sharply raking stems, but typical rounded Dutch sterns. Most of them were sprit-rigged and set flat-headed topsails on to a tapering pole-mast. Most of them seemed to have no standing rigging except the forestay. As far as we could gather they were all shrimping at that time and worked two trawls, one from the foredeck and one aft. Seen in the harbour they looked attractive and tremendously solid and at sea they appeared to be very good seaboats.

We picked up a conversation with one of the fishermen

and he told us that the smaller boats were not paying and were being sold off at twenty-five pounds each. Most of them were going as yachts and were still quite sound and sea-worthy. We were for a moment tempted to pool our resources and buy one to sail home but then thought better of it; very slightly I still regret that caution. In fact the Flushing fishing boats are the only ones I have ever held to be anywhere near to rivalling the Colchester smacks.

The following day we sailed up the canal to Middelburg and brought-up alongside a quay just beyond the town. In the afternoon we went ashore to explore and after half an hour looking in the shops found a café with outside tables where we sat down to drink coffee and watch the street scene at leisure.

All the women were in national dress and the town had an air of open prosperity which was in harmony with the richness of the cathedral bells overhead. We sat on until the shops closed when the streets quickly became almost empty and then made our way back to the smack.

Here we found waiting for us our first English-speaking Dutch schoolboy. They abound throughout Holland and our specimen was typical. A pleasant little shrimp of a boy, who spoke excellent English, but talked incessantly. He was still sitting in the cabin talking just as much by one o'clock in the morning, but by then we had had enough and, picking him up, dumped him overboard on the quay. Here for a time he continued talking to us, but eventually Chaundy in mock rage chased him back towards the town.

At six in the morning he was on board again, but this time Chaundy chased him away in good earnest and thus began a running war between Chaundy and the whole race of Dutch schoolboys. Both sides seemed to enjoy the battle which was fairly evenly matched, though I suspect that the kids had the best of it on a points decision.

From Middelburg we sailed up to Veere and brought-up just short of the lock gates. The village was very quiet but attractive. One of the lock gates was being mended and I went over to watch the men at work. They were dressing it with Stockholm tar and they told me that this was the only preservative worth using. The Dutch government had experimented with all kinds of improvements and substitutes but none had done as well as the traditional tar which had been used beyond memory. This seemed to me to be a convincing recommendation and I have had great faith in the material ever since.

From Veere we locked out bright and early in the morning and with a strong fair wind sailed inland to the Zandkreek through an area of creeks and saltings very similar to Mersea. The weather was fine and the countryside quiet and deserted. It was rather like sailing up a Ray Creek miles and miles long and we thoroughly enjoyed it.

From the Zandkreek we ran out into the Oosterschelde which we crossed to reach the entrance to Zierickzee by about midday. The town lies inland at the head of a mile-long canal which is narrow, but with a fair wind we soon reached the town itself and brought-up against some barges of potatoes lying beside the quay.

Almost at once we were invaded by Dutch schoolboys, but Chaundy took up station on the quay and, arming himself from a heap of potatoes, let fly each time a head appeared round a street corner. This lasted for about ten minutes and then his flank was turned and he found himself under a heavy attack from the rear. He was obliged to retire on board and for half an hour the kids kept us prisoner. In fact they were remarkably good shots and not a few potatoes reached the *Charlotte*'s cabin through the small gap where the slider was out beneath the hatch. Eventually, we decided to brave the fusillade and escaped ashore.

We wandered up the small street to the town square where we found a fair in progress and, pooling our dubbeltjes, decided to put the entire population of kids on the roundabouts for half an hour. The proprietors of the fair entered into the spirit of this and gave up collecting money. For about half an hour we had the pleasant sight of about fifty children in national costume piled on board the hurdy-gurdy with every appearance of enjoyment.

All of the children were strikingly clean with fresh, bright complexions and cheerful-looking faces. Grown-ups and children alike seemed to be totally unselfconscious and we had a feeling of having belonged among them all our lives.

At the end of the free half hour the hurdy-gurdy gave up and stopped. The kids swarmed off and, before we realized what was happening, had surrounded us and joined hands. With a mixture of fun, mockery and good humour, they began dancing and singing round us and this tamed even Chaundy. For a few moments there seemed to be no way of escaping, but finally with a flapping of arms and a mock roar Chaundy broke out and ran. We ran too and a hot pursuit then followed us back to the smack. Here the kids again mounted guard, but later the gathering gradually dispersed.

In the evening we went to a tavern beside the quay and were made warmly welcome. We stayed until well into the night yarning and talking and then eventually retired on board again.

The next two days were idle ones and we simply lounged about. We made several expeditions inland but found precious little room for walking on. Almost every inch of soil was under cultivation and the absence of weeds among the crops showed us that the many people hoeing were doing their work well and thoroughly.

They spoke to us easily as we passed them and seemed quite happy for us to watch them, but none stopped working to talk to us. This impressed me and put me in mind of the old fishermen on Mersea mudflats who would talk to me as a child but never for a moment paused from their winkle-gathering. When not out in the country we idled in the rather sleepy little town and thoroughly enjoyed it.

It was time for us to be on the move again however, as we were by no means over-confident about our return crossing. Quite apart from the question of not having the money to leave the smack on the continent if the weather came in rough, it was very much a point of honour that she should get back on time and in good order. Our plan was to work back in easy stages and, as and when opportunity arose, to take it and get the crossing done with.

We intended to go outside Noord Beveland back to Veere, where we would lie the night, and then next day go outside Walcheren to Zeebrugge. From there we would be guided simply by the weather.

We left Zierickzee at about mid-morning on a falling tide and had a beat to get out of the canal. Unfortunately we ran the smack ashore on the third tack and when we could not pole her off ran the sails down.

An amiable Dutchman motored down in a small fishing boat and stopped alongside. He asked us to pass him a warp. This was not really very welcome as the smack was already well out of her marks and was heeling considerably. We did not think there was any chance of shifting her, but did not wish to seem ungrateful and hurriedly decided to pass the end of the trawl warp which was not strong enough to do the smack any great amount of damage. We would take only a single turn round the bitts and veer out cable until we came to the end of it. However, we had not reckoned on the resourcefulness of the Dutchman.

His diesel was firing about once every second, but when it did fire the volume of sound made it quite clear that it was a very powerful engine. After passing him the warp, we waved that we were ready and he put his engine into gear. We began veering away the warp, but despite our best efforts the *Charlotte* was creaking badly beneath the strain. We were too busy with the warp to be paying much attention to the Dutchman, but suddenly heard the exhaust note of his engine increase in a ringing crescendo of sound which lasted for about a second before he shut his throttle back again.

The warp began smoking on the bitts and Hervey was swearing lustily about our over-helpful friend. To our surprise the smack picked herself up almost bodily and fell outward into the water. The warp came slack as our friend let his end go. He gave us a triumphant wave and then, opening his throttle wide, motored away down the canal putting up a tremendous wash and bow-wave.

More than a little relieved that we were not still towing behind him we set up our sails again and resumed our beating out towards the entrance. This time we paid more respect to the edges of the canal and made our way down without trouble. Outside we had a fair tide and a fresh wind and made a quick passage round to Veere where we brought up on an anchor just short of the lock gates. Seen from this angle it was not difficult to imagine Veere as a strong mediaeval fortress.

Next morning we went ashore together in the dinghy. Hervey and Chaundy wished to revisit the village, but I was curious about the dunes and we parted company for the morning. They were lucky enough to watch a jousting match between rival villages and this I regretted missing, though I had a very pleasant morning on the desolate expanse of dunes. Watching the sand shifting in the wind, I could easily imagine the whole lot moving miles in a single gale.

In the late afternoon we went back on board and got under way to sail round the outside to Zeebrugge. Chaundy was doing the navigation, while Hervey had gone below to try to get some sleep. The idea was that I should take her out of the relatively straightforward entrance and then at midnight he would take over for the hitch from Westkapelle to Zeebrugge.

Before we were barely outside I was beginning to worry about the height of the swell running in and had my hands full keeping steerage way on the smack as she took the combers close hauled. Chaundy was unconcerned and was busily translating the names of the sands we could see. Certainly the rather barbarous names he produced seemed fitting enough. Presumably the sands must have been very steep-to because the swell breaking on them did not seem to run over them at all but instead burst straight upward in a continuous cloud of spray. I decided that at least I was not likely to run ashore without good warning, but for all that the prospect looked bleak and there could be no doubt that we had a rough and dirty night ahead of us.

I had almost too much wind for whole sail, but was having so much trouble keeping way on the smack that I was hesitant to try reducing it. For some reason we seemed to have worked the tide out wrongly and I was making only very slow progress down the coast on a long and a short leg beat. I was happy enough while daylight lasted, but badly wished to get a decent offing before nightfall. My trouble was that on the short tack I was losing almost all my gain down the coast and was worried about being swept back towards the Roompot.

Just after dark Hervey mutinied about the wild motion and came out on deck to grumble bitterly about my habit of cracking on the moment he took his eyes off me. He ran the staysail down and disappeared below again. In fact I could fully sympathize with him. Chaundy and I were both feeling fairly green and what it must have been like in the *Charlotte*'s cuddy I was not very willing to imagine.

The smack was on the short tack when this happened and standing out to sea was for the moment safe enough, but to keep way on her I was having to sail her tremendously full and bye. The old smacksman's dodge of looking as far over one's shoulder as one could to judge where the smack would point on the next tack did not give me any grounds for optimism, and after about ten minutes I decided that Hervey's stomach would just have to lump it. We were too hard-pushed to be lolling about lightly on an unknown lee-shore. I gave the helm to Chaundy and went below to put Hervey better in the picture.

He was remarkably decent about it and said that anything would be better than trying to sleep down below. It was within half an hour of his time to come on deck anyway and he would come out and we would really drive the smack at least until we had weathered Westkapelle. We did this and, with the staysail set again, began to hold up against the tide. Shortly afterwards it turned and began to run in our favour. From then on we made good progress although it was still rough water.

From Westkapelle we were able to bear away slightly and about an hour before dawn reached the shelter of Zeebrugge Mole where we ran down the peak and staysail and reached in towards the red and green harbour lights. We brought-up in the fishing vessel basin. As daylight came we saw the yacht basin on the other side and sculled the smack over to it. We all felt very glad to be in shelter.

Allowing that we were all young and inexperienced, it is still to me something of a mystery that year after year we always contrived to work out the tides wrongly down that stretch of coast and next day we did the same thing again. We put out when we felt sure we should have a fair tide down to Ostend and after about six hours of hard sailing in very rough water we were glad enough to square away and put in to Nieuwport where we gratefully lay the night.

On the following morning we got away early, but ran the smack ashore on an unmarked groin on our first tack across the basin, and on a falling tide went overboard with pillows and mattresses to try to protect the hull as much as possible from the rough stones. Fortunately she sat up well and the water was smooth so that she took very little harm.

After she was dry we changed our clothes and went up to explore the inner basin, and here Chaundy became involved in an argument with the man who hired out the hoop-nets along the quay. His contention was that twice the price could be charged if the proprietor allowed his customers to bait the nets with broken mussels. Eventually the proprietor gave up and went home to lunch, whereupon Chaundy shinned down the wall and collected a shirtful of mussels. These he smashed and let out all the nets baited at twice the usual charge. He put the money in the proprietor's hut and suggested that the time was now ripe for going somewhere else.

We decided to go to the beach and on the way bought some of the canvas smocks worn by the Belgian fishermen which later proved to be a very good investment.

On the beach Chaundy decided to have a bathe and was promptly arrested by a gendarme. We had him released only by pleading that we were due to sail within the hour. We returned to the smack and finding her now afloat with the weather fine, put out and made the crossing to the Foreland without any further delay. In fact it was a very good crossing and none of us was sick at all.

Our departure had been hurried however and we found

that we had very little fresh water on board. We decided to clear Customs at Sheerness and, when the Customs tug had not arrived after half an hour, Hervey and Chaundy launched the dinghy and took the water breakers ashore to fill them. The Customs arrived soon after they had gone and I had a difficult half an hour explaining that, apart from some opened boxes of Dutch cigars, we had no dutiable goods on board though the skipper and third hand had taken the liberty of going ashore without clearing.

Eventually the culprits returned and disarmingly assured the Customs officers that all was well. I was now more or less absolved but I have to confess that I still rather treasure the half hour that followed.

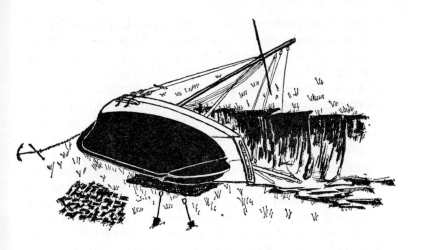

Chapter 18

Some time before the *Charlotte*'s sail to Holland I had finished with my exams and was now earning a modest income which I intended to use fitting the *Teazer* out properly. I had not done anything about this before the holiday, but when we came back went to William Wyatt and asked him to bring her on the hard to recaulk her right through. To my surprise he was unwilling and, when I pressed him, would go no further than to suggest that I brought her into the firm's mud-dock when he would have a look round her and decide whether she was worth my going on with.

The boys I sailed with were unanimously against my going on and told me repeatedly that, although she had been an ideal pastime when I had no money to spend, she was most unsuitable for fitting out in earnest.

This was true but there were three issues involved. I was sure that the job could be done and I was also quite sure that I could do it, but was less sure about the desirability of trying to sail an eighteen tonner single-handed. At that time I felt strongly that single-handed sailing was the ideal. We argued about all this until everybody was sick of the subject.

Independently, the others began looking out for likely buyers, and when a crowd of bearded youths appeared in the Victory looking for a large smack they pounced on them and told them that the *Teazer* was exactly what they were looking for. These youngsters had just returned from the Spanish Civil War and were at once christened 'the Spaniards'. They seemed to be interested and were brought down to Wyatt's to look at the smack. All twelve of them came on board dressed in flowing Moorish robes. I was probably antagonistic and found them difficult to talk to reasonably. Strongly put off by them, my unwillingness to sell the smack became firmer and a whole series of new arguments started.

This was one of my less happy periods and for some time I seemed to be at loggerheads with everybody. In the end I agreed to compromise. I would not sell the *Teazer* to anyone at all, least of all to a crew as humourless as the Spaniards. On the other hand I had no objection to giving her to William Wyatt and he could sell her to anyone he chose. William Wyatt was amused at this suggestion, but accepted it and I heard a few days later that the Spaniards had bought her for five pounds.

Shortly after this someone from Wyatt's telephoned me to say that the Spaniards had let her list into the dock and she had sunk by taking water through her hatches. They had tried to float her by putting inside her several empty beer-barrels which they had borrowed from the Victory. This had not succeeded and they were now talking of abandoning her. Wyatt's wanted her out off the dock before the weight of water inside burst her open and hoped that I would give the Spaniards a hand. I was not optimistic about this but agreed to help.

In the evening I went down and met the new owners at the smack. Of the twelve, all but two declined to do any work, so I dropped them out of the argument forthwith. The two who did agree to help were decent enough and did try, but were hopelessly out of condition and within an hour of starting to dig were more or less exhausted. They stuck it out however and when we packed up at dusk, the *Teazer's* keel was beginning to shift down from the edge of the dock. We arranged to meet again next evening.

We had nearly a fortnight before the next big tides, but after three evenings found that we had got her down enough for her to float. We put in another two evenings and at the end of that she was listing no more than forty-five degrees. The tides had taken off and we bailed the hull out dry and rolled the barrels up to the edge of the road, but there I packed up and left them to it. Next evening the barrels had gone and I took it that they had rolled them back to the Victory. I rather wished that I had been able to watch them do it.

When the big tides came the smack floated without trouble and we remoored her in the centre of the dock. Some time later she was towed away to Maldon to be fitted out as a houseboat and by chance I was walking down the causeway as she left. She was being towed by a Maldon smack and the Spaniards were on board. It did not look convincing and I was unhappy for her, but some months later heard that she had been sold again and was now to become a working smack.

Three years after this she was mined while trawling off Tollesbury Pier and quickly sank, but her crew had time to board their boat and rowed ashore shaken but otherwise quite unhurt.

Parting from the *Teazer* had not been an easy decision and watching her leave Mersea to be turned into a houseboat had made me repent disturbing her in the first place, but when I heard that she had been sold again, this time to a seaman, I hoped that perhaps all had been for the best.

Perhaps a week after hearing this good news I chanced to meet Manny at the top of the causeway and jokingly asked him when he was going to sell his smack to me. To my surprise he said that he hoped it would be soon as he was emigrating to Canada at the weekend.

I had not heard of this at all and at once asked him how much he was asking for the smack. He named his figure and by my standards it was an enormous amount of money. I had my cheque-book with me, however, and although my account was only narrowly in credit I gave him a cheque for the full amount without argument.

I told him that the bank would be more likely to pay it if he allowed me to clear the matter with them and he laughed. I took it that he had agreed and we arranged to go for an acceptance sail on the Thursday afternoon two days ahead.

My knowledge of finance was limited, but I took it for granted that I could raise the money somehow, and on my return home asked my father whether he would be willing to vouch for me during the period it would take me to pay the money off. He was amused at the idea and told me that as I had managed to get myself into the scrape I would doubtless find my own way out of it. I had always got along very well with him and could appreciate that my situation was not without amusement when seen from the point of view of a spectator, but began to realize that my interview with the bank manager next day was not likely to be all my own way. At breakfast next morning the subject was not mentioned, but I noticed that my father seemed to be in excellent good humour.

Towards the end of the morning I went to the bank and, picking on one of my schoolfriends who worked there, asked if I could see the manager. Something in his expression as he told me that this should be possible warned me that Manny had not waited but had already been in to cash the cheque.

I did not have to wait, but was ushered in to see the manager at once. He was holding the cheque in his hand with every appearance of distaste and did not seem particularly pleased to see me. He bade me good morning and then without pause told me very sternly that I was never, and he repeated, never to do this again. He then came round from behind his table and to my surprise almost shooed me out of the door. I took it that all was well and left him willingly enough. I was the owner and master of the *Boadicea* and ever afterwards have thought of that particular bank manager as a very good friend. My father never mentioned the subject but I suspect that he had some hand in the matter.

Next day I caught the lunchtime bus to Mersea and met Manny on the hard. It was a cold windy February day with the wind just south of west. The smack was lying in the Gut and we rowed off to her. We quickly put two reefs in the main and set the storm jib. Under that rig we slipped the mooring and as soon as she was away I set the staysail.

Manny took the helm and sailed her fast out to Deeps, then on to the Nass-end where he brought her on the wind and began beating up the river. He was quiet and moody and I left him to himself. At the start he had been sailing her well but almost unkindly and I could guess that he was not very happy. Now he was beginning to relax. The smack was behaving beautifully and was so small and handy that she might almost have been a dinghy.

We went up as far as Osea where we turned and he gave the helm to me and bleakly told me to get on with it. The wind was well aft and strong, but it was a lee-going tide and the sea was smooth. The smack creamed along with the foam round her stem rising almost level with her rails. Her bow-wave stretched away wide on either side and was unbelievably high for her size.

As we ran further down the river the swell increased and in a quartering sea the smack began to need more careful steering. She was obedient, light as a feather and tremendously good fun.

Manny had hardly spoken during the earlier part of the sail, but now he lay in the scuppers watching and laughed at me openly and gaily as I sailed her. I would like to think that for at least those few minutes he enjoyed the sail just as much as I did.

Back at the mooring he was quiet again and rather formal. He asked me if I had any doubts and I assured him not so, though he knew that well enough without needing to ask. He handed over the papers and wished me luck with her. I thanked him and wished him good luck with his new venture in Canada.

Next day I finished work fairly early, went to the Colchester Custom House and had the smack re-registered in my name. I then continued on down Hythe Hill to Francis and Gilders' ships' chandlers and bought myself some blankets and a chart, two galvanized water breakers, a brass binnacle compass and finally a brass gimball lamp for the cabin. Unblushingly, I paid for these by cheque.

Chapter 19

On the Saturday Chaundy and I took the smack out and more or less repeated the sail I had with Manny, but this time there was a good deal more wind and we decided to leave the dinghy on the mooring. We sailed out into the river under two reefs and, with the first of the flood under us, made a fast and boisterous passage up towards Maldon.

We reached Osea more quickly than we had reckoned on and it was clear that there would not be enough water for us to go much further. Just short of Osea Pier we decided to turn back, but then noticed a squall coming down the river and delayed for one more tack to find out how the smack would behave when it reached her.

We wended fairly well in on the Osea side and then sailed close-hauled waiting for the squall to reach us. There could be no mistaking the weight of wind that was on the way, but it took longer coming than we expected.

We had more than enough time to make our preparations. The topping lift was already to weather, and Chaundy took it up hand-tight. He then took up station by the peak halyard and cleared it so that if need be he could ease the smack quickly.

We began to hear the noise of the squall overhead while the mark of it on the water was still perhaps two or three hundred yards away. At this time we were about half way across the channel. A few seconds later the squall reached the smack and she put her rail down at once, but then felt stiff. She gathered increased way and as she did so began heeling rather less. She was steering easily and answering her helm quickly.

Almost at once she began to take the short seas on board over her weather bow and as her speed increased so the amount of water coming on board became more. I took it that I was driving her to hard and let her luff. The effect of this was that she picked herself up appreciably and lost about half of her forward way, but still took the same amount of water over her bows. Where before the water had been quickly spilling itself away to leeward it now filled her decks and she became sogged with it.

For a fraction of a second I was torn between a sense of disbelief and a regret that the edge of the channel was now so close that I could not continue and find out whether she really was beaten. I was half-tempted to wend to give me time to find out more, but that would put the topping lift to leeward and this decided me. I waved to Chaundy and he ran the peak away. As he did so I brought the helm up to run.

The smack paid away easily and as she came round I gave her more mainsheet, checking it as it went. During the moment when she was broadside-on she was swept fairly heavily, but was heeling again now and the water quickly cleared. A second later she was round, dry-decked, scudding before the wind.

Chaundy came aft and we gybed her and then let her continue running at something near maximum speed until the squall passed on ahead and left us.

While it lasted this was exhilarating sailing and we were both elated at the way the smack had behaved after her helm was brought up. We contrived to ignore the fact that before having the helm brought up she was far indeed from being at ease.

Only years later did I come to realize that for quite the wrong reasons we had unwittingly carried out one of the basic evolutions of seamanship at the exact moment it was needed. This evolution is not taught nowadays and I had not learned it. When the smack began to be overwhelmed I did what I supposed to be correct and let her luff, but by good chance did not have enough searoom to continue doing so and almost at once was obliged to bear away.

Whether or not we could have foundered the *Boadicea* in the sheltered water of the Ware cannot be decided, but I do know now that had I continued luffing I would most certainly have brought her very near it.

That knowledge was not to be mine for another eighteen years, but when the second incident occurred it at once connected in my mind with the first one and without hesitation I brought the helm up and ran, just in time.

Taking the two incidents together, my quick reaction to the second one makes me believe that our sense of elation as we ran down the river came from a background knowledge that we had escaped disaster only by good fortune.

The wind was still strong and we let the smack run on with her peak rucked away until we reached the Nass where we reset the peak for the fetch up Deeps. We then carried on back to the mooring without further incident.

Shortly after this sail I went down to the smack one Thursday lunchtime. The wind was light southerly and the tide at about half-flood. I set the whole mainsail and big jib and after clearing the halyards let the mooring go. I then walked aft to put the helm down to check her as she paid away, but to my surprise the helm was dead and the smack made no attempt to answer it.

Instead she continued to pay away until she had the wind right aft and then began to move forwards. She was now heading towards the shoal water on the point of Ray and, as her keel began to 'smell the mud', the flood tide through the

Gut swept her head round even further. Before I realized what was happening she gybed all standing and ran herself ashore.

This was dreadful. Even had I been in the privacy of some deserted creek I would have been ashamed, but here I had made an exhibition of both the smack and myself in about the most public part of the whole estuary.

There was nothing that I could do about it now except carry on and get the sails down as best I could, but this was by no means easy as the topping lift was to leeward and both sails were full of wind. Somehow I did get them down and took the kedge anchor off to weather in the dinghy. Returning from this I sat on the smack's rail to wait until she floated and in the meantime tried to work out what I had done wrongly.

Try as I liked I could not see that I had done anything to deserve such a disaster. The whole thing had been carried out at leisure in exactly the way I intended, but I was quite sure that there must be some simple mechanical explanation. In default of anything more convincing I decided that perhaps the big jib had overpowered her and accordingly unbent it. I then set the small storm jib in its place and, when the smack floated, tried again under this new rig. I found that she sailed out of the creek perfectly easily and was no trouble at all.

As soon as she was out in the river with room to make mistakes I hove-to and changed back to the big jib to find out whether it did show any sign of overpowering her. I found that she was perfectly at ease with it, had good weather helm and wended easily. This was reassuring, but it did nothing at all to clear up the mystery of her unexplained gybe.

Everybody in Mersea knew about the gybe but saw only the amusing side of it. Repeatedly I was told that it would do me good and the smack had done it only to show her independence. This was an explanation which I did not accept and I felt quite sure that there was somewhere an unsolved problem which would one day find an answer.

Eventually the smack did the same thing again but this

time I understood what had happened and the problem was solved.

The incident occurred during the winter when several of the boats were ice-bound. For this reason I had a crew of skippers on board so that things were done rather too casually. The smack was lying in Thornfleet and the wind was fresh westerly with the tide at about half-flood. We went on board and slipped two reefs in the main, but decided to do without a jib, so that this time there was no question as to whether or not it was the jib which had overpowered her.

Two of the boys hoisted the mainsail, cleared the halyards and then set the staysail. One of the others waited until the staysail was up and then let the mooring go. At the time he did this the smack had just ramped up to the mooring and snubbed and she was lying idle in the water. Her helm was dead and she had no steerage way. Her head payed off and her helm was powerless to check her. She continued to pay away until she had the wind right aft and then, pointing directly at the Middle Ooze, she began to answer, but it was too late. Before she could come round she had sailed herself ashore. We ran the sails down and laid off a kedge, and then went below to light the fire and wait until she floated. I was not greatly put out about her behaviour because at last I understood what had happened when she made her unexplained gybe in the Gut a year or so before.

Simply, unless a vessel has steerage way she cannot answer her helm and can only pivot round her centre of lateral resistance. The time to let a mooring go, or come to that the time to break out an anchor, is when the vessel is ramping up to it. During that period she is carrying helm and will answer, but after she has snubbed she is lying idle and is out of control until she drops back and pays away again.

That much was obvious at once, but beyond it were other things, some of which took years to work out fully. These are technical things and the less directly-concerned reader can perhaps usefully skip the rest of this chapter.

When a sailing vessel is hard-pressed in a seaway she needs someone who can predict what she will try to do and know

175

why she tries. Given this kind of knowledge she can be helped. The *Boadicea* had just showed me that she weather-vaned to leeward or, to put it more succinctly, she lee-vaned. This was a possibility which had not occurred to me and I had before taken it that any vessel which carried weather-helm also weather-vaned.

The *Charlotte* weather-vaned strongly and, if allowed to come up to wind without way on, would get in irons and then hang in irons until her mainsail was run down. When we were first learning how to sail her we supposed that if we let her gather stern-way with the helm amidships she would break away later when given full helm, but in fact this never did make her pay away and we concluded that when making a stern-board her weather-vaning was stronger than her helm.

At first we were critical of this and felt that the ship-wrights had overdone their efforts to make the fishing smacks weather-vane, but when Bruce fell overboard we revised this opinion because we knew that on several occasions fishermen had been washed over but had succeeded in getting back. We could see that a smack's ability to lie head-to wind indefinitely could well be life saving. It did not occur to us that the survival of the smack might also depend on it, but now with this new evidence of the *Boadicea's* lee-vaning much more of the picture began falling into place.

During the period since I had first owned her I had sailed the smack in the firm belief that she would stand up to any sea and wind in reason, though in the back of my mind I had not entirely forgotten her overwhelming in the Osea squall, and realized that there are conditions in which even the best vessel can founder independent of stranding or collision.

Apart from the one occasion of the Osea squall there had not been any three-reef weather, but several times when moderately pressed under two reefs I had been concerned with the smack's habit of paying away heavily to leeward after wending. At the time I had found this unaccountable and had thought it inadequate to accuse her slightly raking stem as being cause. Now I began to realize that quite as much at fault as her raking stem was her nearly upright sternpost. In fact, the combination of the two made her centre of lateral resistance a good deal further aft than the *Charlotte*'s

In smooth water the smack could be relied on to carry her forward way through wending, but in any sea heavy enough for her to be pitching very much when passing through the wind she lost her way and came round with her helm temporarily slack and idle. When she did this she sagged away to leeward and for a moment lay in the trough before picking up way again. At that time I had not known her to miss stays and fall back on the same tack, but later I found out that when she needed scrubbing she sometimes did miss stays in a heavy sea.

In contrast, the *Charlotte* with her heavy weather-vaning wended easily. Not only did she come up to the wind more sharply when her helm was first put down, but when through the wind's eye was at once ardent even as her sails began to fill. There was no suggestion of her lying in the trough while she picked up way.

I began to understand why the Colne shipwrights had given the counter stern smacks straight stems and heavily raking stern-posts, and from there began to appreciate that if a vessel lee-vanes she must always be worn round rather than wended when beating in a heavy swell under hard conditions.

This knowledge did not all come at once and in any case really hard sailing is the exception, and it was several years before I arrived at a definitive way of managing the smack when she was unduly hard-pressed. In effect what I came to do was to wend her in the ordinary course unless she was obviously ill at ease, in which case I wore her round and found that this was very easily done.

Since she could be relied on to lee-vane heavily when she lost way, I needed only to let her luff and then, just before she lost all her way, bring the helm up so that she paid away on the same tack. I then lashed the helm half up and as she paid away went forward and rucked the peak down until the gaff would pass below the topping lift. I then belayed and went aft to gybe her. After the gybe I lashed the helm half up again and went forward to reset the peak. The smack would meantime come up to wind and continue sailing close-hauled until I had returned aft to take the helm again.

This evolution could be done single-handed in well under two minutes and cost almost no ground to weather. In hard conditions it was less of an ordeal than wending and needed no great exertion. The method also had the advantage of keeping the topping lift always to weather so that if need be the vessel could be eased while sailing without need for coming round on the other tack. The gybe with a reefed sail and the peak run well down is a relatively trivial matter. The evolution is in fact a way of box-hauling done with fore and aft rig.

Even when I had established all that to my satisfaction, I still did not realize that during periods when emergency is likely the topping lift should never be to leeward in a lee-vaning vessel. This as I mentioned briefly when discussing the Osea squall I learned only years later.

To put it in a slightly different way, I still believed that when overwhelmed a vessel can be safely luffed to ease her. This is taught to all youngsters when they are learning how to sail, but is in fact no more than a misleading half-truth.

In moderate conditions of wind and sea the teaching is well enough, but beyond that there are extreme conditions in which luffing will involve shipping serious amounts of water while the vessel is upright and cannot spill it. If she is a weather-vaning vessel she will hang in irons and take no harm, but if she lee-vanes she will hang in irons for perhaps a second and then quickly pay away to leeward sogged with water and with half her stiffness gone. During this period she may well be laid on her beam-ends. Far better to ease her by rucking the peak and bearing away while she still has steerage way. In brief a lee-vaning vessel is in peril if she gets in irons because she cannot be relied on to stay there.

Paradoxically, there is one situation in which any vessel, weather-vaning or lee-vaning, can be relied on to hang in irons when least convenient and that is when she has been incorrectly broken away from the hove-to position.

When a vessel is hove-to she will answer her helm slowly and can be made to bear away, but if her headsails are allowed to draw before she has been made to do so the situation is different. Now she will not bear away at all, but instead bluffs her way up into irons with her helm slack and idle. In fact this is about the only way the *Boadicea* can be put in irons, but given the chance she will do it every time.

What I think is happening is that the vessel is making as much leeway as forward movement while she is hove-to, and driving through the water in this crabwise manner the thrust on the bluff of her lee-bow is greater than the thrust on her tapering after-body. This preponderance of thrust forward makes her luff although she is not carrying enough forward way to answer her helm at all.

I call this lee-bow luffing, or more briefly 'bluffing', and it seriously detracts from the usefulness of the hove-to position, particularly when working in narrow tideways.

Under such condition, unless one takes an inconveniently long time making sure that the vessel has really picked up enough steerage way before her headsails are allowed to draw, one cannot rely on her breaking away quickly to wend and be hove-to again on the new tack.

Even in the lee-vaning *Boadicea* this problem of bluffing has been so much nuisance to me that later on I evolved a modified way of heaving-to with the peak run right away and the helm lashed hard down. When it was necessary to change tacks, the smack was easily worn round instead of being wended and I found that this was a much more reliable way of managing her in hard winds when pre-occupied with clearing a trawl in narrow tideways.

Chapter 20

The *Boadicea* had been sold with her boat but without her mooring and without any of her fishing gear. I lay her out in the mouth of Deeps and for some weeks used her simply as a yacht, but this I soon found to be an empty way of sailing and quickly became bored with it.

At first I had no crew, but later began having a crew on Sundays although I usually went out single-handed on the Saturdays. This worked out quite well, but it was clear that soon the smack must be found some fishing gear and I made inquiries in the Victory. I was told that the *Waterwitch* was giving up and I was lucky to buy her sixteen-foot beam-trawl at a purely nominal price. Charlie Hewes found me three oyster dredges and rigged them and I then bought myself a thirty-fathom trawl-warp of three-inch bass, together with three ten-fathom dredge-warps. With this gear on board the smack was fully equipped again and on the following Saturday I set out to make my first attempt at putting her to work.

On the *Charlotte* I had been well trained as to how to sail the smack but our trawling, even after two years, was still on a make-learn basis and we had worked together as an informal committee. I had never attempted to put a trawl over single-handed and had never thought out in detail for myself the order in which the various moves should be made. I now had to remedy this omission and by the time I set sail on the Saturday I knew at least what I intended doing.

The morning was fine with a fresh easterly breeze and I had a lively beat down the river with about a score of other smacks. One or two were large smacks from Tollesbury, while the others were divided about equally between the small smacks from Maldon and the rather larger ones from Mersea. Lower down the river two Colne smacks also joined the fleet. This in fact was the last occasion on which I saw any sizeable number of smacks trawling under sail close together. On the way down to the Knoll where I knew that the others would put-to we were all beating under whole sail and the *Boadicea* was trimming easily so that I was able to leave the helm untended for quite long intervals.

The wind was slightly touching off the north shore, so I cleared the trawl in the starboard scuppers and after making sure that there were no twists in the net made fast the cod-end buoy line which closed the bag of the net. I then cleared the bridle and rove the trawl-warp through the bridle-block, taking the end forward outside the rigging to make it fast round the barrel of the windlass. The coil of the warp I cleared on deck ready for letting the trawl go. When this was all done to my satisfaction I went back aft and carried on sailing the smack, though in fact she needed precious little steering.

The other smacks were still more or less in a cluster round me, and taken together in the bright sunlight the various colours of their tanned sails made an exciting and realistic background for a first trawling expedition.

When it came to the time for putting-to, I decided that since I was by no means sure about how I was going to manage, it would be sensible to carry on beyond all the others so that in the case of trouble I would not be in anybody's way.

When well clear of them all I eased the helm down to put about from port tack to starboard and at the same time threw over the cod-end buoy. I then began clearing the net over the rail until it was all out. The smack was now just coming through the wind's eye and I lifted the forward trawl-head over the rail and slewed the beam across the smack's quarter. In theory all this was excellent, but in practice I was far too slow, and before I was ready the pull on the net streaming out to weather took the beam over the side willy-nilly. I decided to accept this and paid out the trawl-warp slowly until the net reached the bottom. For a moment or two I felt the vibrations coming back up the warp and, since all seemed to be well, I belayed.

Although very raggedly executed, this was not too bad for a first attempt at putting-to single-handed and later on I learned to do it properly. In the meantime I had at least put the net over and it felt as though it were still the right way up. I straightened up to look round to find out what the other smacks were doing.

I found that I was still well clear of them and well up to weather, but I also noticed that while putting-to they had all slipped in two reefs. I was still under a whole mainsail. This meant that unless I did something about it I would be towing much faster than they were and would inevitably tow right through the whole fleet. My plan for keeping clear had gone astray. For some reason it did not occur to me that I could still easily reef without upsetting the way the trawl was towing. I decided to carry on and tow through if reasonably possible, but if collision or fouling seemed likely I would run the sails down at once and haul.

On this basis I let the smack carry on and as she drew up towards them, the crews of the other smacks were helpful. Each smack in turn shifted her warps so as to tow clear of me to the side and make room for my wild career between them. Each crew I passed gave me much good advice and humorous comment.

The last smack of all was the *Sibyl* and I expected something more severe from her skipper, as he was noted for outspokenness. As the *Boadicea* surged alongside he straightened his back and gave me a cheery wave. Like all the other fishermen he had powerful lungs, and with a tremendous voice he called out, 'Ride 'em cowboy'. He then gave me a huge grin and turned away to make some further adjustment to his warps. He paid no more attention to me after that, but his cry was taken up by the crews of all the other smacks and for a few moments the river echoed to catcalls and laughter. There was nothing to be done except wave back and join in the laughter with them.

I was now through and clear and had open water ahead of me so I was able to complete the rest of the tow without anxiety. I hauled at the Bradwell 'metes' which marked the beginning of the forbidden ground belonging to the Oyster Company and was delighted to find that although the net had been towing much too fast it had fished well and contained a bumper haul of soles.

A few weekends after this first haul, the fish left the river and I went out to try to find them further out down the Wallet. The weather was again fresh and easterly and after putting-to below Clacton Pier I towed for about half an hour. I then found that the pull on the warps was becoming too heavy and knew that something must be amiss. I ran the sails down and began to haul the net in. It was very heavy pulling and only with great exertion was I able to bring the beam up to the rail. I was unable to lift it inboard but made both ends of the bridle fast to hold the beam while I paused to take stock of the situation. The net was filled solidly with jellyfish.

If this were to happen now I would simply take a knife and cut a hole in the net large enough to let the unwished for catch go clear, but at that time I had not yet learned how to mend nets properly and worried about spoiling the trawl. I set to and bailed out the jellyfish until the weight was enough reduced for me to get the net safely back on board. During this period the smack drove herself broadside along the coast and was nearly back to the Nass before I was clear.

This was well enough on a fine day with the wind blowing me home all the time I worked, but it would have been more difficult in westerly weather and I decided that the trawl was too heavy to be worked easily alone.

That was fairly obvious, but the problem of how to

remedy the matter was not so easy and I debated it with myself for some time. I had no wish to make the trawl-heads lighter, nor did I wish to cut the net down and possibly spoil the set of it. In the end I decided to cut two feet off the length of the beam thus reducing it to fourteen feet. Somewhat to my surprise I found that this was most effective and the trawl became much easier and lighter to manage. As far as I could assess it, the cut-down trawl fished just as well as it ever had done.

Later on when the net wore out I replaced it with a new one nine score meshes wide across the head instead of twelve score and this again seemed to fish just as well as had done the bigger net.

After the catch of jellyfish the trawling was more or less ended until the autumn and I brought the smack in to make ready for the holiday which I intended to take in Holland. She was repainted and scrubbed and laid-off the weekend before I was due to start.

For this holiday I shipped a largish crew, but decided against trying to go direct as the weather forecast was light variable with local thunderstorms. Instead we crossed the estuary and made Ramsgate by the Saturday evening. On the Sunday we crossed to Dunkirk, but had light winds and calms all the way though quite a heavy swell was running. During the calm periods the boom was unmanageable and the slamming about of the gear was so heavy that several times I was obliged to lower the mainsail and lash the boom and gaff to the rail as securely as I could. Even this was not very satisfactory and the amount of chafe was heartbreaking despite sacks lashed round the parts at risk.

Eventually we brought-up about a mile outside Dunkirk and laid the night to an anchor rolling very uncomfortably in a heavy thunderstorm. In the morning a small breeze got up and soon after dawn we managed to fetch into the harbour and lay alongside a pilot cutter. We were all fairly exhausted and had a lazy morning on board.

The pilot cutter belonged to an elderly yachtsman who was now running her as a charter-boat and we were amused when, an hour after we had brought-up alongside, a dozen or so schoolgirls emerged from her hatches. They all departed ashore and I had an hour yarning with her owner.

He showed me his mainsail and asked me to guess how old it was. The sail was of heavy tanned flax, but it was beautifully soft and flexible. I guessed it as being ten years old, but he told me it was more than thirty and had been in more or less continuous use. He told me that he had it regularly re-dressed with fish-oil and ochre mixture. The halyards were about twenty years old and were of best quality tarred Italian hemp dressed each year with the same mixture. I had a look at them and found them to be still sound and tightly laid though soft and pliable. He pointed out to me that working boats all had the fall-ends of their halyards secured so that they did not untwist and lose their lay. I had not before realized the significance of this.

His gear was a convincing demonstration of the virtue of good dressing and I have myself used either tallow or fish-oil dressing each year ever since, but have come to add a small quantity of red antifouling to the ochre and believe that this improves the dressing.

Later in the day we put out from Dunkirk and beat up the coast in light airs to reach Ostend in the late afternoon. We went in and laid the night there, but were out again early next morning to carry on to Flushing. Our early start did us little good however and after a short time I was obliged to anchor and was astonished at how fast the smack began going through the water the moment her anchor checked her backward drift.

By about midday the tide turned in our favour and we set course again to beat along the coast in a light but steady breeze. During this part of the sail we were in close company with a Royal Yacht Squadron gaff cutter and I felt almost envious of her. She was in fact a very lovely boat and everything about her gear was obviously as near perfect as was possible. Tack and tack we sailed together and I watched her two professional hands closely as to how they sailed her. They wended her with consummate artistry and each time contrived to get her round and away with barely a sail ruffled. This was a first-class lesson for me and, very much on my mettle, I tried hard to sail the *Boadicea* just as well. Provided she is really clean, the *Boadicea* has a surprising turn of speed in smooth water and light airs and she held the yacht tack after tack all the way up to Flushing. We both locked into the Middelburg Canal and lay alongside the quay.

After we had stowed the smack's gear and made all ship-shape I sat for a time on the quay and the owner of the cutter came down and passed the time of day. He told me that during the sail up the coast he had very much admired the smack and very kindly said that it was a pleasure to watch a smack being sailed properly. I admitted that the sailing he had admired had been no more than blatant imitation. This amused him and he said that he had already more than half suspected it, but no less credit on that account.

Needless to say I was tremendously proud of this, but nearly a year later, was even more proud when the same yacht with her White Ensign flying from the peak, hove-to beside the *Boadicea* while she was trawling in the Blackwater. Her owner called across that he was still envious and was glad to see that someone still took enough interest in fishing smacks to go out trawling under sail.

Next morning the wind was very light and we towed the smack by mast-head line and found it easy enough taking turns to walk the warp along the towpath. Chaundy was among the crew and had the warp when the kids from Middelburg cycled down the path to come and meet us. They at once recognized him and ragged him about being a horse, which was not wise, because as a student we had some-times called him 'horse'. However, since he had the towrope to keep him quiet the kids had it all their own way and made the most of it.

In fact, everywhere we went the kids at once recognized Chaundy and at Zierickzee he was fairly mobbed. His em-barrassment was comical to watch.

We made much the same visits as we had done in the

Charlotte during the previous holiday, but made two additions. One was up the long narrow canal to Stavenisse and the other was up to Willemstad. At Willemstad the weather changed and from there we had stronger winds. During the beat back from the Zandkreek to Veere we chafed through the second reef-pennant, and blew out the storm-jib, but I am afraid that neither of them had been very honest.

The weather continued rough and we came back down the coast in short hitches to make the final crossing from Ostend.

Chapter 21

After the holiday I took part in the autumn trawling. Later, when the colder weather started, I brought the smack in to a mooring in the Gut to give her a thorough clean-out below decks. When Wyatt's had put in the new topsides and deck some years before they had not shifted the lining in the cabin and this I now stripped out. It was a good decision and having seen the mess there was behind it I would not now willingly put any kind of fixed lining in a boat.

The wood behind it was sodden wet and the spaces between the frames were filled with sludge. The lining had probably been put in when the smack had been reframed and replanked some fifty years before, and it was clear that the shipwrights had allowed any amount of rubbish and shavings to fall behind it. This had now rotted down to provide a home for woodlice and a species of whitish wood-boring grub. These I later found out hatched out each summer as brownish-coloured flies which breed freely.

After cleaning the rubbish out and scraping down all the spaces which had formed between the planking and the frames I burnt the whole area dry with a blow-lamp. All the surfaces were then treated with a flowing coat of green Cuprinol and when that had dried I painted them. This proved to be ineffective treatment, however, and the smack was never clear of the woodlice or the grubs until I eventually rebuilt the entire hull twenty-five years later.

Looking back I think my attempts to dry the wood and then impregnate it with an oil-based preservative were bound to fail, and I might have done much better if I had stuck to the old-fashioned method of laying dry rock-salt on all the bad areas while they were still damp, and then repeating this until the wood was thoroughly brined.

This refit took most of the winter and was tedious work though I had a good deal of help from various friends. We came out again in time for the spring trawling and had good fishing but did not extend our range beyond the usual grounds in the Blackwater, Wallet and Raysand.

During the summer I decided to take the smack to Holland again despite the fact that the war seemed likely fairly soon. For some time crisis had followed crisis, and at each of them it had seemed that war was inevitable, but each time the issue had been evaded and there was no reason to suppose this situation would change. Allowing that war must come in the end it seemed sensible to try to steal one last visit to Holland before it did come. Not everyone agreed with me, but Chaundy said he was game to come and we thought that the two of us could manage without further crew. We left the final decision to the last moment and then, as no new crisis had arisen, set out late on the Friday to take the ebb out to sea.

In light winds we made slow progress and lost the tide soon after going through the Spitway. For the first hour of the flood we were nearly becalmed, but then a breeze began from the north-west and soon increased to a fresh whole-sail wind.

It was a clear, fine morning and far away down Swin we could see something white which at first we could not recognize. We then realized that one of the square-rigged Grain Ships from Ipswich was coming down Swin towards us under full sail. I had sometimes seen various of these vessels brought-up below Ipswich Docks, but this was the first and only time that I ever saw one at sea. We bore away slightly to try to intercept her and to our delight she eventually passed very close to us. She was in ballast, heeling quite heavily and, at the time, we estimated she was doing about twelve knots.

While she was approaching, my attention was taken up with the overall picture that she made, but as she came nearer the vessel herself and the lofty area of sail lost importance and became only a backcloth to the man standing on her poop looking down at us. He was a thick-set man of middle age and, watching him, something made us decide that on no account should we wave. We called up good morning to him and then the vessel was quickly past. We commented that whoever the man was he had, at least for that morning, no rival and seemed well able to carry the distinction.

The wind continued fresh and we kept up to the north of the Galloper intending to go direct either to Flushing or the Roompot. The sea was rising and, with the wind on her quarter, the smack was rolling heavily. Irritatingly we both began to feel seasick. There was no reason for this and in equally rough water at home we would neither of us have even thought of being sick.

Possibly the beginnings of seasickness made us careless. The dinghy was on deck and we had pushed the chart loosely under her stern. One fold of the chart began to flap but we took no notice of it. A moment later the wind caught it and the whole chart was whipped overboard. We saw it floating white side uppermost and wended at once, but there was too much surf for us to see it and we realized that we should have put a marker buoy out as soon as it had gone. Eventually we gave up the search and bore away again to carry on with our passage.

We had lost the only North Sea chart we had and decided that we must now change our plans so as to be reasonably sure of making a landfall in daylight. The leg to Flushing was rather too long to trust and we altered course to the south to make the crossing shorter.

By mid-afternoon we picked up the Belgian coast and identified Ostend. The tide was setting to the west more strongly than I had reckoned on and, to my discomfiture, I had to make a double gybe in the entrance to get in. Once inside we brought-up and made fast alongside a lighter.

I had not seen Chaundy since our previous holiday and we had much to talk about. Secure in the belief that in a foreign port no one would have much interest in our conversation, we sat on deck talking shop. Some subject arose on which we did not agree and we argued the matter. While we were still involved in this, a gentleman appeared alongside in his dinghy and apologized. From his yacht opposite he could not help but hear what we were arguing about and had rowed over to tell us that in fact we were both wrong.

We all laughed and we invited him on board, where we introduced ourselves. This was Christie Ray a colleague of whom we had both heard, but had not met before and we spent a pleasant evening yarning and swapping ideas. He did not have a spare North Sea chart and was fairly sure that we should not be able to get one on shore until the Monday. We went over to look at his chart and memorized the bit between Ostend and Flushing. He had just come from Holland and had visited most of the places we knew. We yarned again for a time and then parted company fairly early as we all wished to turn in in good time so as to be fresh for the morning.

On the Sunday the weather was unsettled, but the wind was still north-west and fresh. We set out at about midday and, without any navigation troubles, reached Flushing by early evening. We locked into the Middelburg Canal and lay the night alongside the quay.

On the Monday we made a tour of all the likely-looking shops in Flushing looking for another North Sea chart, but did not succeed in finding one. I wrote home asking for a new chart to be sent out to us care of the grocery store beside the quay. We decided to spend that evening in Flushing.

On the Tuesday we ran up the canal to Middelburg, where we stopped and spent the afternoon partly for the pleasure of listening again to the cathedral bells. Later on we went back on board and ran the rest of the way up to Veere where we lay the night. In the morning we locked out and sailed inland round to the Oosterschelde and brought-up on an anchor off Ouwerkerk.

During the night the weather deteriorated and we woke to find a moderate gale blowing from the south-west. I had no barometer on board, but had been half-expecting this and thought that probably there was worse to come. We decided to carry on up the Krammer Gat and had a rather depressing sail in cold, wet, rough conditions. I had intended to carry on if possible as far as Willemstad, but Chaundy, who was doing the navigation, was attracted by a village which he said was called Dintelsass and we put in to find out what it was like. The place proved to be a huge rectangular basin without any sign of human habitation within miles.

We brought-up in solitary state and then sculled the smack over to the weather wall and made fast alongside. The basin looked so bleak and deserted that, had the weather not been so foul, I would have put out to go on again.

We had a meal and afterwards as the rain had now stopped we went ashore to go for a walk along the dyke. There was no sign of a village and after about half an hour we turned back. The wind was beginning to drop and by the time we reached the smack again the sun was shining. Although cool, it was now quite a pleasant evening.

About an hour before sunset barges began coming in and we sat on the wall watching them, sometimes giving a hand with the warps as they eased themselves in beside the wall. The barges were all motor driven now though several of them looked as if they had only recently changed from working under sail. Without exception they seemed to be crewed by a whole family and most of the couples were fairly young. Usually there were two or three smallish children on board and, as they came in, it was the housewife who had the helm while the husband and children made ready with the warps on deck.

As barge after barge came in we realized that on board all of them the pattern of life seemed to be very similar. The girl at the wheel was still in her apron and was fairly obviously in the middle of getting a meal ready, but was handling the barge with skill and confidence. They were not by any means all the same, but all of them seemed to have in common a complete lack of artificialness. Strangers though we were, they were quite unselfconscious while we sat watching them. The kids and the menfolk were nearly all in very clean blue overalls and everyone seemed to be full of energy. As each barge came in it was rather as if a new guest had arrived at a party where everyone knew each other well.

Several of the elder children could speak English and at once picked on Chaundy. We gathered that none of them went to school, but instead picked up school books and set exercises at each port they came to and then handed in the completed work at the next port on. It all seemed to be very vigorous and efficient. We found ourselves envying what seemed to be a very useful and worthwhile way of living.

What had been a miserably deserted basin only half an hour before was now become a very busy and pleasant little Dutch town. The activity and bustle did not last for very long however, and by dusk not only the kids but the grown-ups too had all disappeared below and had presumably turned in. We guessed that 'early to bed and early to rise' was the general pattern of their existence. Before turning in ourselves we took coffee and cigars on deck and sat for a time talking in hushed voices in case we disturb the silent fleet of barges round us. It seemed to us that there is something worthwhile about any community which by common consent turns in when the sun sets.

Next morning we heard the barges begin getting under way before it was barely light and turned out to watch them go. Only the menfolk had turned out and, single-handed, each cast off and edged his barge out of the basin and away. By the time it was full daylight the last of them had gone and we again had the basin to ourselves.

We had a fairly early breakfast and then lounged until tide-time, undecided as to our plans for the day. My original idea had been to carry on up to Dordrecht, but in conversation with the barge-crews the evening before we had gathered that some new crisis was in the offing. If this were so it might be sensible not to get the smack tucked away too far inland.

We seemed to have two alternatives. Either we could take the ebb down and make our way to Zierickzee, which we both wished to visit again or, if we wished, we could run up to the Helle Gat and then work back towards the coast through the Haringvliet. Hellevoitsluis seemed to be well situated for making a quick get-away if need-be.

This second alternative had the advantage that it would allow us to see the Helle Gat in rough weather and this we both wanted to do. On our previous visit to Willemstad it had been chiefly the fierce-sounding name of the Helle Gat which had attracted us, but on that occasion it had been disappointingly tame. Judging by the amount of wind we could hear overhead, we thought that this time it certainly should be more exciting.

We decided to leave about an hour after high water which would allow us to reach the Helle Gat at a time when the ebb should be running at about its hardest. From the Helle Gat through to the Haringvliet there were two channels and the most northerly one had the advantage of being called the Voile Gat, which sounded just as exciting as the Helle Gat itself. On the chart the Voile Gat looked very narrow, but with luck it should be a fetch and in any case there should be a strong tide in our favour. We decided we would attempt it. For some reason it did not occur to us that Hellevoitsluis was also a fairly impressive name.

It was now about half-flood and we decided to go for a short walk ashore. Although lying sheltered close in against the wall we knew the weather was fairly rough, but when we climbed the iron ladder to the top of the wall we were slightly subdued by the amount of wind we found there. I had of course noticed many times that wind on shore always seems worse than when on board and under way and we trudged off for our walk without being unduly worried. We arrived back half an hour later and then lounged until it was time to go.

An hour after high water we set up the two-reefed mainsail, with the full staysail and the storm-jib. Getting out of the basin was no problem and we set off on our run towards the Helle Gat. We were quite unaware that over all this area the water is barely salt at all and is much more easily made rough than seawater. Not knowing this we merely remarked that the ebb tide was kicking up an imposing scuffle but, running to leeward as we were, this was no trouble to us and the smack was sailing easily.

In due course we opened the Helle Gat and here the spectacle really was imposing. Across the whole width of it short, steep seas were jostling each other in a wide vista of wind-torn surf. Even with the wind aft it was fairly wet work sailing through it. The smack was still comfortable, however, and eventually we hauled our wind to stand in towards the Voile Gat. Now we began to take more water on board and quickly found that the smack was not pointing as high as we had hoped she would. From the outset it was clear that we should not make a fetch of it through the Voile Gat. However the tide was obviously boiling along in our favour and we thought that on a long and short leg beat we should have no serious trouble.

I was a bit concerned about the wending at the end of the short leg as the channel was very much narrower than we had thought, but decided that if we missed stays we could always run back with the mainsail rucked away.

The first few tacks were exciting but in a way the excitement was more visual than real and we remarked that, although the sea running would have done credit to trysail weather, the smack was quite at ease with two reefs and was not even putting her lee rail down. It was an unwise comment.

With no warning at all that we noticed a squall swept down and the smack began to lie over to it. Within ten, or perhaps twelve, seconds of the squall starting, the kedge anchor was washed overboard and had I not watched it happen I would hardly have believed that such a thing was possible while sailing in sheltered inland water.

Watching this anchor being washed overboard was part of my education. The anchor itself was a smaller model of the main bower, but was more heavily built. It was in fact a good anchor with short flukes and a thick-set shank and crown. It weighed ninety pounds. When stowed it had one fluke outboard of the rail just abaft the starboard jib-bollard. The shank lay at right angles to the rail and the stock rested inboard on the deck. I did not keep this anchor lashed in the ordinary course because it did not seem conceivable that it could easily shift, let alone wash overboard.

The first sea of the squall shifted the crown about a foot aft down the rail and the second sea did the same again. The third sea came over the weather bow and swept the anchor outboard. As the sea drained clear of the deck one end of the anchor's stock was visible jammed against the rigging.

Chaundy went forward to try and save it, but was unable to pull it back on board against the pressure of water. He turned and waved to me to luff, but this I could not do, partly because the vessel was too hard pressed and I had far too little room to manoeuvre if I allowed her to lose way, but more immediately, because I was worrying about the movements of a tug approaching from the other end of the Voile Gat. She was already uncomfortably close and it was essential that I maintain steerage way.

The ring of the anchor was under water and short of a serious risk of going overboard with it there was no hope of making a rope fast to it. In any case Chaundy looked none too secure where he was and I waved to him to let go and come back aft.

During the few seconds he had been struggling with the anchor I had realized only too clearly that if he should get washed overboard there would be no hope for him at all, even though the shore was no more than a hundred yards to leeward. He was in fact a strong swimmer, but I do not think that any swimmer could live for more than a few seconds in the short, steep sea which runs while a squall is at its height. I was very glad to see him come back safely aft again.

Meanwhile the tug had stopped a short distance ahead. She was easily the largest tug I have ever seen and, judging by her name which was in an alphabet we could not read, we supposed her to be an ocean-going Russian salvage tug. It was obvious that she could not possibly get past while we were in the channel and I wended to take a short tack over to weather where I intended to drop the anchor and bring-up.

While we were crossing the channel we signalled that we intended to anchor, but a figure came out to the wing of her bridge and waved his hands horizontally as though to say that this would be no good. At the same moment the tug began to go astern fairly quickly. I had no desire to run myself ashore on a falling tide even on the weather shore and, as soon as the tug began to go astern, I wended to give myself more time to think about it.

If she could go astern there was no reason why we should not do the same and I waved that I would run back to the Helle Gat to let her through. The figure on her bridge again waved his hands horizontally as if to say no good. The tug increased speed and very quickly drew herself backwards out of the Voile Gat leaving the way clear for us. At this point the squall eased and left the smack sailing in a normal two reef wind.

The sea did not abate so quickly and for a time the smack continued to take water heavily over her bows. She was heeling enough to spill it easily but was no longer seriously pressed and we had enough leisure to watch the tug make her way out to the more open water of the Haringvliet. Here we expected her to wait until we had got through to clear the way for her, but to our surprise she made no pause at all. She turned round and at what looked like full throttle motored away out to sea.

What kind of speed she was making I can hardly attempt to guess but I would think not much less than twenty knots. Outlined against the white of her own bow-wave rising high before her she looked magnificent. Quite probably we were intended to be impressed and certainly we were.

Chapter 22

In due course we reached the more open water of the Haringvliet. Even here the amount of sea running was impressive. After making two tacks the wind began freeing us and soon we were able easily to fetch close in down the weather shore. The smack was becoming hard-pressed again however and it was clear that the wind was backing and increasing. Unexpectedly, the sun broke through and the effect was to bring out the peaty colour of the broken water most strikingly. We commented that it looked Dutch enough to please anybody, but was wetter than proper water.

The wind was still backing and increasing and the smack was now making so much leeway that although she was looking well up to windward the gain to weather was very small indeed. I began to realize that I must on no account let her get down to leeward.

In the Voile Gat a moderately heavy squall had not impaired the smack's ability to turn to windward, though it had worried her by greatly increasing the roughness of the pent-up weather-going tide. Here in the shelter of the weather shore the sea, although wet, was not a serious embarrassment and it was the wind itself which was troubling her. I know now that for this part of the sail she would have performed better with three reefs in the main and a reefed staysail.

In the distance we picked up the entrance of Hellevoitsluis well down to leeward, but I was far from trusting the situation and continued to keep up to weather as much as possible. Hellevoitsluis was at the extreme edge of our chart and was shown as a small town with a canal leading away to the north. We supposed that this would be similar to the canals which lead up to Zierickzee or Stavenisse. Foolishly it had not occurred to us that it might be a canal with lock gates.

My chief worry was that the entrance lay on the lee shore and I decided to hold away until I had opened it and could see inside, but this raised problems because the ebb tide was still setting strongly down the Haringvliet and, if I left it too late to bear away and run in, the tide would set the smack so much up to weather that I would have to gybe which would involve making a second gybe as I took the entrance. In the present weight of wind this was a complication to avoid if possible.

Under easier conditions I would possibly have gybed and then run the peak down as need-be so that I could approach crabwise across the tide to make an easy rucked-mainsail gybe at the entrance, but pressed as the smack was I decided to go just far enough to allow me to look inside, and then if the entrance were clear I would take it at full tilt. The peak and the staysail could be quickly run down the moment I was safely in. In effect I had arrived at the theoretically correct answer to the problem. To take a narrow entrance on a lee-shore in a strong tide it is sensible to keep all sail set until one is sure of getting in.

Having reached that decision it was obvious that the final difficult run in should be made as short as possible consistent with being able to claw away if the entrance should be obstructed. I began freeing the smack away so that by the time I could look inside she would be perhaps three hundred yards out from the end of the breakwater.

As we opened the entrance and could see that it was clear, I brought the helm up and in order to counteract the tide ran the smack as nearly dead before the wind as I reasonably dared. At first this looked as though it should give me a margin in hand, but it soon became clear that the smack was still being slowly set to weather. At the distance of about a hundred yards out I very nearly changed my mind in favour of making a double gybe rather than go further towards sailing by the lee, but bearing away another degree or two managed to keep her on the required line of bearing. Even so she won a little and soon I was able to luff back a trifle which made the steering very much less worrying.

During the run in I was too occupied to pay much attention to what the harbour looked like inside, but did have time to notice that beyond the entrance the canal was closed by lock gates. As we entered I called to Chaundy to run the stay-sail down but told him to leave the peak alone in case we had to luff quickly to bring up.

From a distance we had seen a fair number of masts and had supposed that inside there must be some kind of fishing-vessel basin. For this reason we did not pay much attention to a nearly empty ferry-dock which we opened on the starboard side, but almost at once saw that there was no second opening.

It was already too late to gybe and enter the ferry-dock and ahead of us lay a cul-de-sac with the lock gates at the end of it. We had run full tilt into a trap.

The ebb tide was three-quarters spent and the canal ahead of us had shelving walls of rough stone. I guessed that the navigable width was just over two smacks' lengths. Had the width been even three lengths I would almost certainly have risked a wending, but running in at the speed we were it was obvious that wending was out of the question in the width we had. For a fraction of a second I debated running the smack ashore on one bank or the other, but a glance at the rough ragstone walls convinced me that if I did she would simply rip her bottom out.

Conceivably there was still one way in which the smack could be turned. I had never tried it, nor even thought of it before, but the idea came fully formed. I called to Chaundy to run the jib down willy-nilly and come aft to help me gybe. He waved and I knew he had guessed what I had in mind.

Speed was essential but he had one thing to help him. The fall-end of a smack's jib halyard is secured to the forward starboard shroud and cannot unreeve or lose itself. All he needed to do was to throw down the coil and cast off the belaying from the cleat on the stanchion. The sail would then run itself down with no further need for his attention.

Without delaying to watch him, I turned and began to haul in the mainsheet quickly hand over fist and had it three parts in by the time he came aft to help. Between us we bowsed it home straight up and down, exerting the utmost strength we could muster. Above all we needed the mainsail to set flat. I left Chaundy to belay and turned to give my full attention to the steering.

The lock gates were still some distance ahead and for the moment we had time in hand. I carefully eased the smack over to weather until she was as close in as could be risked. For a further moment I held her steady and then gave her full helm as harshly as was possible.

The smack gybed at once and, since she had been harshly flung into it, the mainsail filled solidly with wind while it was still coming over. Even with two reefs in the sail the impact was sickeningly heavy. For the first time in my experience of heavy gybing I kept the helm hard over instead of checking back. Despite the weight of the wind I did not expect her to be laid fully on her beam-ends to shift her ballast, but I did hope that she would lie down far enough to skid bodily to leeward and by so doing lose her forward way. There was nothing for it but to trust that I had judged her actions rightly.

When she first lay down she took the water well up on her deck and began skidding broadside-on, but was also pivoting as the pull of the mainsheet drew her stern round. As she came round to lie more head to wind she began to pick up and right herself.

The reefed mainsail was set high, so that the length of peak halyard between the blocks was small and the peak of the bowsed-in sail sagged to leeward very little. The sail was setting flatter than I had dared to hope for and there was almost no forward drive in it.

During the first quarter of the turn the smack forereached appreciably and by the time she was broadside-on she was already well over on the far side of the canal, but as she came more head to wind and began picking up she was still skidding to leeward and was in effect now making a sternboard. She had come very close to the stone wall but now, moving aft down the line of her keel, she drew herself away.

As soon as she was round far enough for the staysail to set to weather Chaundy hoisted it and sheeted it flat on the port bowline. For the moment the smack was being leisurely in her movements and he had time to coil and stow the halyard while she was coming head to wind.

I called to him that I would look after the bowline while she wended if he could go ahead and reset the jib which during the gybe had been trailing in the water from the bowsprit-end. The halyard block was still hooked in to the head of the sail and the sheet was still belayed to starboard as it had been when he let the halyard go. To reset the sail involved only hoisting it and belaying and then coiling and stowing the halyard.

While he was doing this I stayed aft until the smack was just through the wind's eye, when I cast off the mainsheet and overhauled it by about a fathom. I rebelayed it and, as the smack payed away on the port tack, lashed the helm half up to free me to go forward and let go the port bowline so that the staysail could blow to leeward. Usually I would have followed the sail across the foredeck to secure the lee bowline on my way back to the helm, but Chaundy was occupying that part of the deck and I left the bowline for him to deal with when he was done with stowing the jib halyard. I went back to the helm along the weather deck.

The smack was picking up forward way by the time I

reached the helm, and freeing it I steadied her to sail close-hauled to windward. Chaundy made fast the lee-bowline, so that now she was shipshape and under control.

The port tack was the shorter of the two and if anything I wended early. The smack answered easily and came about in the slick of smooth water she had left behind her as she was skidding down to leeward. On the second board we wended short of the ferry-dock entrance, but on the fourth one weathered it and bore away to sail in.

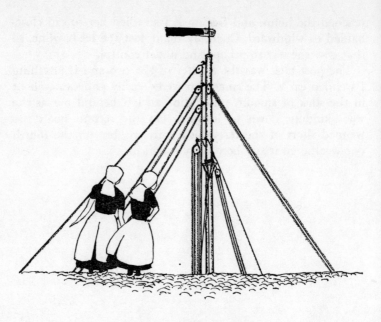

Chapter 23

Inside the ferry-dock we were out of the wind. We dropped the anchor fairly well out from the weather wall and lay to it while we ran the sails down and stowed them. We then sculled the smack over to the wall and made fast alongside.

Sailing a relatively small boat in strong winds is so exacting that the extent to which the wind itself is tiring is easily overlooked and only when one reaches shelter, or perhaps heaves-to and goes below, does one realize what a physical relief it is to be out of the continuous noise and buffeting. While we had been outside in the Haringvliet neither Chaundy nor I had been aware of tiredness, but now we were inside and sheltered by the wall we both felt too lazy to go below to put a kettle on. We commented on this and both admitted to having hoped that the other would find the energy to do it. We agreed to give ourselves a five minute rest while we lounged on deck to light our pipes and relax.

There was no need to talk. We were both aware that largely by fluke we had hit on the only way there was of getting the smack round without wrecking her and we needed time to think the thing through again and digest it properly.

Three officials came along the top of the wall and we supposed that they had come to collect the usual harbour dues. In fact they wished us to shift and for the moment we both felt unwilling. We could not speak Dutch, nor they English, but we pointed to the dial of Chaundy's watch and tried to convey to them our willingness to move out in an hour's time. They shrugged their shoulders and went away down the wall again. We decided that they would probably come back before long and thought it would be sensible to go below and have some kind of meal before we did shift.

We found that, everything considered, the cabin was still much tidier than we expected it to be and we lit a primus to heat up some soup. From outside we heard the sound of a heavy engine starting and at once went on deck to find out what was happening.

The ferry had cast off from the staithing on the far side of the basin and was motoring slowly towards three piles set in a cluster just ahead of her. We watched with interest while she carefully nestled her bows against the piles and then realized what this meant and what was going to happen. At once we realized just how idiotic we had been in refusing to shift when politely asked to do so.

When the ferry had snugged her head securely against the piles she opened her throttle and, using full rudder, began to swing her stern out across the basin. Behind her the water boiled in a wide swathe which spread out towards the entrance of the dock. At present the wash was streaming well clear of us, but as the ferry swung it would come round, and within a few seconds we should receive the full weight of it at close range.

The anchor which was fairly well off seemed to be our best hope, and while Chaundy cast off our warps I hove in chain to take the smack clear of the wall by about a fathom. On a scope that short there was little hope of the anchor holding when the wash reached us but there was no time to shift the smack now and we could only wait and improvise as best we could.

The wash swept slowly round towards us, but just before it reached the smack two things happened at the same time. The rebound wave running towards us along the wall caught the smack's stern and swept it round to lie further out and at the same moment the ferry cut her engine. Afterwards we guessed that this was the way the ferry crew had planned to do it and, to give them their due, it did not work out at all too badly.

Although the ferry was no longer making new wash, the old wash continued to swing round towards us and it reached the smack's bows a fraction of a second after the stern had been swept out from the wall. The bows were swept in until the smack was lying broadside-on and then she was surged in bodily. Meanwhile the rebound wash coming back from the wall surged her from the other side and she rolled heavily. The main wash was the stronger and she was swept in against the wall, but the rebound water took a good deal of the weight out of the impact. We fended her away as strongly as we could and nearly held her though she took one blow which shook her badly.

For a few moments the smack continued to roll, but the wash was subsiding now and she was no longer in danger. We picked up the warps we had cast off and made fast again.

The ferry had continued swinging after her engine had been cut and was by now fully round. She started her propeller turning again and began to motor out slowly. On her deck she was carrying cattle and a few people, but on her bridge we saw our three Dutch officials looking over towards us impassively. We looked back. Chaundy who had his own sense of fun waved to them and they waved back, and then we all laughed. She quickly drew away behind the wall on her way out to sea, and for the time being we had the ferry-dock to ourselves.

That was fair enough, but the ferry was bound to return soon, and we were quite sure that we had no wish to be still in Hellevoitsluis when she came back to do the same thing again. We thought that with luck we had about two hours before she was likely to come back and went below to begin again getting ready our interrupted meal.

As we expected, the soup had overturned, but we quickly put on a fresh lot and added meat to it to make a seagoing stew. The dock remained quiet and we finished our meal in peace. After clearing up the crocks we lounged for a time and then went out on deck to set up sail and make our escape.

Outside the harbour we found that the wind was still strong, but nothing like what it had been in the morning and the tide which was now running to leeward made the sea smooth. With a fair wind we sailed back towards the Voile Gat.

I was tempted to go into the Spui, which on the chart looked attractive, but its general direction was to leeward, and beyond what the chart showed us of its mouth we had no information about it. We had had enough of adventure for one day and decided to play safe and go back to Willemstad. We would lie the night there and then next day begin working back to windward with the idea of making Zierickzee in perhaps two tides.

The wind was taking off and by the time we reached the Voile Gat it died away altogether, but the tide was sweeping us along at a good speed and we simply let the smack drift. When we reached the Helle Gat we began sculling and, with both of us at work, made our way fairly easily across the fairway to reach the Willemstad entrance. We sculled the smack through into the basin and brought-up beside the cobbled road.

The evening was dull and rather chilly, but after the rough day was pleasantly quiet. We both felt too lazy to bother with going to the town and instead took coffee and cigars ashore and found a seat on the quay opposite the smack.

A few yards in front of us the smack's mast rose above the level of the quay and Chaundy pointed out to me that below the hounds where the chafe of the gaff-jaws came, the wood was worn away to about half its proper thickness. He thought that I might have been a good deal less cool about the gybe before Hellevoitsluis lock gates had I known that the mast was in that worn condition.

This was certainly true and I had not before known that the amount of wear was anything like so bad. We roused up and went back on board where I rigged a bosun's chair to go aloft and examine the damage closely. Seen from this angle it did not look so alarming and, reassured, I came down again. Even so, it was clear that a new mast would need to be put fairly high on the list of necessary repairs and in the meantime it might be sensible to nurse the smack along rather more gently than we had been doing.

Chapter 24

The lull in the wind did not last and during the night I heard the smack straining to her warps while the wind and the rain gusted round her. When we turned out in the morning the prospect was not attractive and we gloomily watched the trees inland bending and swaying while the smack's rigging shrilled to the note which I associate with two reefs and wet decks. Outside, the Helle Gat was a torment of broken water and looked discouraging to say the least of it.

It seemed to us that the foul weather had set in in good earnest and was not likely to make any quick change for the better. We decided that when all was said and done the Helle Gat and the Krammer Gat were sheltered waters. We would leave at tide-time and make as much gain to weather as we could while the ebb lasted. We ran out under the staysail, and as we cleared the entrance set up the double reefed mainsail and the storm jib.

Although fairly hard-pressed the smack behaved well and wended easily, which was just as well because any number of motor barges were taking the ebb down with us and during the whole sail we were constantly needing to juggle with our tacks in order to let them through. Sometimes this was difficult, but without exception the barge crews were good-natured and tolerant. None of them hooted us impatiently, but if need be hung about astern until there was room to get by and then dashed through cheerily tooting as they went. The smack was keeping us too busy for us to be much worried about being a nuisance to everybody, but we did find time to enjoy the enthusiastic waving from the kids on board as each barge in turn speeded up to dodge past.

After a long but quite satisfying beat, the tide turned against us and we put into a barge haven for the night. During the evening the weather fined a little but by next morning was just as bad again and under similar conditions to the previous day we beat down to Zierickzee. Towards the end of the sail it began to rain and by the time we bore away to enter the canal we were not sorry to be out of the rough water. We were both tired, but Zierickzee was a home away from home and, after bringing up alongside the quay, we stowed the gear and went ashore to visit the tavern where in previous years we had always been made warmly welcome.

To our surprise, as we entered the bar the room became obviously hushed and we drank our beers feeling uncomfortably aware of the awkward silence. After a mere ten minutes we said goodnight and took our leave. Outside along the quay we met a friend of previous years and for a few moments stood and yarned with him. He seemed to be worried about us being there and we went back on board feeling thoughtful and depressed.

On the Sunday we lay in until the afternoon and then turned out to find that the weather was still vile. We had a short walk ashore but the town was bleakly deserted and we soon went back on board. We rummaged out enough wood and coal to light the fire which made the cabin much more snug and cheerful. We settled down to read, with coffee and cigars handy. By evening time we both felt more cheerful and decided to stay on board rather than go ashore again.

On Monday the weather was better and we spent part of the day in the town sightseeing. We did our shopping and found that most of the shopkeepers remembered us. They seemed glad to see us again though we both thought that they were more restrained than they had been during our previous visits.

Finally we went into a jeweller's shop and bought some small silver spoons to bring home. The jeweller was not restrained at all and told us that he was glad enough to sell the spoons and anything else we wanted. He told us in so many words that if Holland were occupied, his chances would be slender indeed. We walked back to the smack feeling far from happy.

In the evening we decided to brave the tavern for a second time and on this occasion found the men less reserved. We did have some conversation with them and gathered that the only thing worth talking about was the likelihood of war and Holland's occupation. As far as we could assess it, no one doubted that Holland would resist invasion but there was a strong difference of opinion as to whether the local population should resist.

Later on at home when England seemed likely to be invaded a similar mutual distrust was evident in rural populations, but this we did not know then and the situation worried us. We both felt that we were idle spectators of impending tragedy with a holidaymaking role which was out of place and an embarrassment. When we left we made our farewells and said that we should be leaving in the morning. We both had the impression that everybody was relieved that we were soon to be on our way.

On the Tuesday we set sail some time before high water and ran back to the Zandkreek. We then had a hard sail back to Veere where we locked in. The wind direction would just allow us to fetch down the canal and we decided to take the opportunity while it lasted. We carried on and brought-up alongside Flushing quay just before sunset.

Troops were patrolling the quay and had every appearance of taking their duty seriously. Perhaps ten minutes after we had brought-up, two harbour officials came down and told us that we could not stay. The lock would open at midnight and we must go out on the tide.

This was disconcerting and I pointed out that we were both tired after a long day sailing. It would be unreasonable to turn us out into the North Sea on a dirty night in our present state and in any case we had no chart until I could pick up the one which had been sent out to the grocer-store. Unwillingly the officials agreed to leave us alone for the night, but we were to leave without fail next morning. The lock would open again at midday and we must be ready to leave.

Chaundy had not taken part in this exchange, but as the officials left he said that it would not surprise him if they changed their minds and later came back to turn us out that night. It would be sensible if we got some sleep while we could. I agreed with this and after a quick meal we turned in.

We did not discuss our rather brusque reception at Flushing and both misconstrued it. We were both unfamiliar with the protocol of war and failed to distinguish between the personal aspect we had seen at Zierickzee and the official actions of government which now confronted us in the more formal port of Flushing. Quite falsely, we supposed that the desire to get us quickly away stemmed from the same reasons in both towns.

Contributing to this misunderstanding was the earnestness of the troops on the quay beside us. Most of them were boys of our own age and we were very conscious that while at home a policy of appeasement and 'peace in our time' had seemed only moderately shameful it was quite out of place here and clad in our slacks and plimsolls we felt ourselves to be flippant outsiders worthy only of being got rid of with the least possible delay.

Next morning we were up early and as soon as the grocery store opened I went over to collect the chart. To my dismay I was told that Edgar Digby in the *Port Errol* had seen it on the counter two days before and thinking that we were ahead of him had picked it up to take home and give back to us.

This was a quandary. We had searched Flushing for a new chart the week before and it seemed pointless to search again. We went back on board and from the *Almanac* began to compile a list of latitudes and longitudes from which we could construct a rough chart of our own. It was hurriedly done, on the back of another chart, and it was very rough, but it did at least give us approximate courses and bearings, and as need be we could add further information. We decided that we could manage and went out on deck to enjoy our last few hours in Holland.

Chaundy became involved with a bystander, who wished to show him how the local fishing boats stepped their masts strongly enough that they had no need for standing rigging. I let him go on conditon that he should come back well before midday, but knowing his carefree way of doing things watched him go without feeling very confident.

Further inshore along the quay there was a small English yacht and I went down to talk to her owner. He let me have a look at his chart and told me that he too had been warned that he must leave without fail on the midday tide. He was bound for the Crouch and all being well would make the passage direct. I debated doing the same, but decided that my wisest plan was to work back down the coast and leave the crossing to the last moment, when the uncharted distance would be less.

I left him and went back towards the smack where I was met by some different port officials who told me that the lock was being opened and the smack must leave at once. There seemed to be no alternative and, with the help of by-standers, I cast off the warps and began towing her down towards the lock.

To my great relief Chaundy now appeared and with my immediate worries thus solved we locked out. We slipped out our reefs and set sail to begin boating down the coast. For the first leg we sailed with the yacht, but soon dropped her astern and parted company.

As usual down that stretch of coast we had trouble with the tides and found that the ebb out of the Wester Schelde gave us very little help. We made slow progress and by evening time had reached only as far as Nieuwport. We had had enough of it and decided to reach away in and lie the night in comfort.

In fact it had not been a notably pleasant sail. Ignominiously pushed out from a country for which we both had strong ties of affection we had been almost surly with each other. To add to our discomfort the smack had sailed with a complete lack of zest and, with too little wind to steady her, had made heavy going in a blind, lumpy sea. The whole holiday had ended in a mood of black depression.

We made fast to the quay just inside the entrance to the fishing vessel basin, and went below to have a meal. Afterwards we walked up to the town and each bought another of the canvas smocks we had found on our previous visit. Soon after dark we returned to the smack where the harbour master was waiting for us. He told us that we must leave at once.

This seemed to be too much altogether and we were both truculent. We were doing no harm to anyone and we were not enemies of Belgium. We could see no reason at all for being turned out. The little Belgian became voluble in explanation. Certainly we were not enemies. On the contrary we were friends. That was the problem. If England should declare war, which she seemed likely to at any moment, he would have no alternative but to intern us. Belgium was too small and too vulnerable to take liberties with International Law. If a messenger came down to him this moment to say that England was at war he could do no other than arrest us. He had no power to make us go, but go we must and quickly, before it was too late.

This put the whole thing in a different light and at last we understood the unexplained urgency at Flushing. Feeling both contrite and happier we easily agreed to go. He stood on the quay above us as we set up sail and then threw our warps down to us. We pushed the smack's head out from the wall and sculled her across the basin. The sails filled and we wended and then drew out into the dark entrance. The harbour master followed us round the corner of the quay, and stood for a few moments alone in the night wind. The lights on the quay lit up his figure against the wall of darkness round him and I had a strong desire to take him with us. We called out our farewells and he called back.

We cleared the entrance and, pitching as she felt the swell, the smack shipped a sea across her bows. The North Sea was not inviting, but at least there was wind enough, and on a guessed course for the Galloper it lay just forward of the beam. The smack picked up way and we began the crossing.

The night was dark which is unusual at sea, but the swell was long and easy and the smack was sailing fast. She felt purposive and ardent. Neither of us talked much, but took turn and turn about at the helm, each busy with his own thoughts.